CHRISTIANITY AND CULTURE:

A CHRISTIAN PERSPECTIVE

ON WORLDVIEW

DEVELOPMENT

WILLIAM VALMYR, PH.D.

xulon
PRESS

CHRISTIANITY AND CULTURE

Christianity & Culture:
A Christian Perspective on Worldview Development
by William Valmyr, PH.D.

Printed in the United States of America

Library of Congress Control Number:
ISBN 978-1-60791-941-4

www.xulonpress.com

ENDORSEMENTS

—ɯɯ—

""My people perish for lack of knowledge..." (Hosea 4:6). With only 4% of adults equipped with a Christian world-view that informs their decisions, the soul of the nation hangs in the balance. Dr. William Valmyr's practical and scholarly exposé of Christianity and Culture is a potent antidote to the poisons of ignorance and secular humanism that have become pervasive in our culture. Here is a book for leaders. And not just for the classroom, but for the pulpit and the pew."

Bishop Darlingston G. Johnson, D.Min.
Bethel World Outreach Ministries, Int'l
Silver Springs, Maryland

"Dr. William Valmyr has developed and written a compendium of key thoughts, persons and historical events that impact Christians in today's world. While the book can be of help to many disciplines, it is specifically geared toward the educational enterprise.

As an academic administrator and Professor of Christian Education, I believe that this volume will be helpful to seminaries, universities, curriculum developers, home schools, public and private schools and parents.

The structure of the book is designed in such a way that it answers the questions necessary to form an educational philosophy: What is the nature of the learner? What is the role of the teacher? What is the content of the curriculum? What is the purpose of schooling?

While the writing style is more academic, scholarly and research oriented, it is very clear and understandable to reach a much wider audience.

William Valmyr has made a great contribution to the literature of Christian understanding and ministry."

Kenneth Mayton, Ed.D.
Director, D.Min. Program
Oral Roberts University
School of Theology and Missions

"This book is not just another piece of literary research put together to fill pages, it's a unique, thought-provoking compilation of Dr. Valmyr's knowledge, expertise and extensive research showing the connectivity of the elements that make up worldview studies. It provides an understanding of culture, and a thorough explanation of why Christian education must be transformed to cross all cultural barriers, so people all across the world can adapt to a more improved life-changing understanding of Christianity and Culture. Transforming a secular worldview can only be accomplished by understanding the Word of God and how it integrates with education. This book will allow you to embrace change for a brighter future, not just in the religious and higher learning institutions, but ultimately, in the world!"

Bishop Henry Fernandez
Senior Pastor, The Faith Center Ministries
Chancellor/CEO, University of Fort Lauderdale

"Dr. Valmyr has given the church a book on Christian education that is a compelling call to action. Beginning at the beginning with Moses, the Bible requires the education of each covenant generation in truth and obedience. The secular world too, from Plato to Rousseau to Dewey, has recognized the culture determining role of education. Somewhere along the way, however, Christians have forgotten this. They have forgotten that a Biblical view of education must go beyond educating the mind and also address the training of the soul. The secular world has failed at both. It falls then once again to Christians, who founded the great universities and popularized education of the laity to begin with, to take on the role of cultural educator once again. Dr. Valmyr gives us a compelling survey of the background to today's crisis. Integrating the disciplines of history, philosophy, theology, and education, he gives us a glimpse of where we have come from and suggests the place we should go. I hope it gains a good readership, for the task before us is immense."

Warren A. Gage, Th.M., J.D., Ph.D.
Associate Professor of Old Testament
Knox Theological Seminary

"Dr. Valmyr has written a book which is destined to provoke Christian Educators to evaluate their curriculum design. This book is relevant not only to educators, but to anyone who desires to change the secular worldviews in society.

Dr. Valmyr's passion to infiltrate humanistic and pluralistic society in education with the Christian worldview is influenced by his revelation that God created this world and that He deserves to be the center of all our educational systems. This is possible if Christian Educators will approach scripture from a new perspective and with new questions, to discover a new aspect of the DIVINE WORD in regard to education.

This book answers some haunting questions as to why there is moral decay in society and I thank Dr. Valmyr for his scholarship. Indeed, any individual who transmits knowledge based on the understanding of Creator God and His grace will produce balanced students who are capable of going into the entire world and making an impact."

Dr. Nicku Kyungu Mordi
President and CEO
I GO Africa for Jesus Movement and
Africa Transformation Embassy

This book is dedicated to
my wife Marsha and daughter Meghan,
your love and support are
gracefully felt.

"As you therefore have received Christ Jesus the Lord, so walk in Him, **7** rooted and built up in Him and established in the faith, as you have been taught, abounding in it with thanksgiving. **8** Beware lest anyone cheat you through philosophy and empty deceit, according to the tradition of men, according to the basic principles of the world, and not according to Christ. **9** For in Him dwells all the fullness of the Godhead bodily; **10** and you are complete in Him, who is the head of all principality and power."

Colossians 2:6-10

CONTENTS

—₥—

Foreword

—w—

Finally, a definitive book on the Christian worldview needed in academia that is distinct, concise, and comprehensive. Dr. William Valmyr's "no frills" approach gives interesting insights to the difficult questions that are in the heart of Christian America and makes him a "first" among the new generation of Christian apologists. The book outlines key elements in educating to produce a Christian world view.

Our nation has moved far away from its roots in many ways. Dr. Valmyr's solutions are not always easy, but they are given with such powerful conviction that they may forever change our educational institutions. He has formulated a new paradigm, a moral compass, if you will, to navigate through the minefields of theological and political correctness within the contexts of our educational systems.

I Samuel 16:7 says, "...man looks on the outward appearance, but God looks upon the heart." When I meet someone, no matter how brilliant or successful they may be, I want to know their heart. Through the years I have come to know Dr. Valmyr's heart, I can say that this book successfully communicates the very essence of his heart and practice. Best wishes to you, Billy, on a piece of work that raised the bar for the one thing we need most – truth!

Rev. Mark D. Boykin
CMI, Founder and President
Senior Pastor, Church of All Nations
Boca Raton, FL

ACKNOWLEGMENTS

—⟋⟍⟋—

The idea for this book first came to me from my involvement in the educational enterprise at various levels, starting with my participation as a lifelong learner, academic/ career advisor, youth mentor, minister and Christian educator. During the ten to twelve years of my educational journey as both an undergraduate and graduate student, I came to the realization that higher education in America, has had, and continues to have, a great impact on the worldviews in our culture. As I began to do research, I could not help but notice how the minds of most Christians are filled with the philosophies and worldviews of the secular world, even though they were inside the Church! It was then that I went back to the Scriptures, and the words of the Apostle Paul in Romans 12:1-3 and Colossians 2:8 echoed in my soul. Those very words are relevant for today: "…And do not be conformed to this world, but be transformed by the renewing of your mind, that you may prove what is that good and acceptable and perfect will of God…" (Romans 12:2) and "Beware lest anyone cheat you through philosophy and empty deceit, according to the tradition of men, according to the basic principles of the world, and not according to Christ" (Colossians 2:8). These scriptures led to a review of early church history and the historicity of Christian education. As I studied, I noticed the correlation between the cultural conflicts that the early Church faced (internal and external opposition) and the conflict of worldviews in our time. According to Church history, Rome conquered the world militarily, but it is said that the Greeks conquered Rome intellectually. This is precisely what has been occurring in America and the western world for the past century. America has conquered the world militarily for the cause of freedom, but has lost the greatest battle of all, that of the minds and souls of what was once considered a Christian nation. In many ways, the moral decline and ethical scandals that we have recently heard are all a result of our acceptance of secular humanism and secularism as a nation. Consequently, the infiltration of various human philosophies is evident in our schools, our courts of law, our scientific endeavors in medicine, our culture as a whole and even within the fabric of our churches and houses of worship.

It is my hope that this book would serve as a catalyst for change and an antidote to the current trends in our society beginning in our educational institutions. Human philosophies and secular world-views are often propagated through the mechanism of teaching and learning. No society has ever experienced change (transformation) without the active contribution of Christians within the moral fabric of the culture. Jesus commanded us to, "Go therefore and make disciples of all nations ... teaching them to observe all things that I have commanded you" (Matthew 28: 19 – 20); and He said to "...Do business till I come" (Luke 19:13). If you have been inundated by humanistic, liberal and secular indoctrination, the redemptive solutions in this text will ensoul the tools necessary to produce a Christian worldview. This book will impart a commanding sense of purpose, passion, and appreciation for the teaching profession. With heartfelt gratitude, I would like to take the time to honor those who have labored tirelessly in planting seeds of encouragement into my life. The faces of countless friends, Christian leaders and mentors have been before me as I wrote this text. I am indebted to the works of various Christian scholars, authors and great apologists like Dr. Ravi Zacharias, Dr. Jack Hayford, Dr. Josh McDowell, Dr. Norman Geisler, Dr. Warren A. Gage, Dr. Samuel Lamerson, the late Dr. C.S. Lewis, Dr. D. James Kennedy, Dr. J. Rodman Williams, Dr. Ronald Nash, and countless others. Their lives instructed me, opened my mind and deepened my interest in the Christian life. In addition, many have read parts of this manuscript, commented on it, and have offered support and encouragement when the road to finishing it seemed long and difficult. I especially wish to acknowledge all of my mentors and colleagues who volunteered their time and provided counsel during this study. The opportunity to dialogue with Christian professionals in churches, Para-church ministries and higher education (secular and Christian institutions) was a gift I felt honored to receive.

Finally, I want to acknowledge my lovely wife Marsha for her prayers, support and encouragement during the writing of this book. She gracefully accepted the time that I spent in front of a word processor and kept the faith. I thank God for those men who have labored as overseers of my soul, the Rev. Mark D. Boykin, Rev. William "Mike" Griffith, Rev. Marc Kulczycky, Dr. Joe Flores, Rev. Willie Likekele, Dr. Darlingston Johnson and the late Dr. George Fabre, Sr. I am also grateful for my friends and colleagues Dr. Henry B. Fernandez, Ms. Chloris Underwood, Mrs. Dollie Parker-Owens and Mrs. Brigette Broxton for their professionalism and encouragements. Mrs. Rebekah Stevens read with an English teacher's eye, made the book better from first to final proofs and for that I am grateful. I want to express my deep appreciation to the publisher and the editorial team for believing in this project, supporting me during the length of time it took to complete it, and for demanding a high level of excellence. Finally, I would like to thank the countless students that have taken my courses over the years; they embraced my teaching graciously providing their unwavering commitment to learning, constructive challenge, and creative affirmation.

William Valmyr
Margate, Florida
Summer 2009

PREFACE

—⚬—

Christianity and Culture:
A Christian Perspective on Worldview Development

*C*hristianity *& Culture* will consist of short introductory-level chapters in various topics related to the development of worldviews. Although worldviews in higher education have been discussed at length in postsecondary educational literature, it has not yet received similarly intensive scrutiny in Christian educational literature. Our academic institutions of higher learning (both religious and secular) have either explicitly or implicitly influenced the current philosophy of religion in our culture. This philosophy is one that embraces a theology that denies the existence of Almighty God and that has evolved into an age of pluralism, secularism, and occultism.

This book is an examination of the relationship between worldviews and higher education. Many educators, parents, and higher education policy makers in the Christian community remain insufficiently informed about the theory and practice of faith-learning integration and its potential ramifications for 21st century students. This book outlines several key elements in educating to produce a Christian worldview that includes an evaluation on the nature and dimensions of faith-learning integration in both the theoretical and applied disciplines across the curriculum.

William Valmyr
Margate, Florida
Summer 2009

PART ONE

INTRODUCTION

INTRODUCTION

—ᵐ—

Overview of the Book

Why another study on education, Christianity and Culture? Education and worldview development are at the heart of every civilization and play a fundamental role in the culture of every society. If we assume an interest in the role of education in cultural formation and worldview development, we must explore the subject within its historical, philosophical, religious and sociological foundations.

In recent decades, institutions of higher learning, established to educate and train individuals for Christian service, have created a humanistic and pluralistic society that is inundated by secular worldviews. What is being taught in the academic departments of our colleges and universities? How can Christian educators integrate spiritual life within their academic expertise and theological understanding? These are some of the probing questions that have been raised in the evangelical community.

Studies have shown that the gospel message from the early years of Christianity has been misunderstood, misrepresented, and taught through various heretical or unscriptural methods (e.g. the Antinomians "those who perverted the grace of God"). Our academic institutions of higher learning (both religious and secular) have either explicitly or implicitly influenced the current philosophy of religion in our culture. Unfortunately, this philosophy is too often one that embraces humanistic theologies that deny the existence of

Almighty God and have therefore denied the power of the gospel. Consequently, non-Christian education as we know it has evolved into an age of pluralism, secularism, and occultism, and is therefore in need of a spiritual invasion or, as I like to call it, the infiltration of the Christian worldview in education and culture.

The historical root of education cannot be understood merely in our current lifetime nor can it be viewed solely within the confines of what is taking place within the walls of schools nationwide. We are remiss as educators if we fail to recognize that what is happening educationally is the result of the current philosophy of our culture.

Since the beginning of human history, the greatest thinkers of the ancient world, namely philosophers, have increasingly influenced the educational systems of the world. The historical context and philosophical theories of every human era have developed into our current worldview of life. This study is designed to examine the developmental process of spiritual formation through biblical, theological, educational, and religious training. The factors that influence the spiritual IQ of unbelievers as well as the spiritual growth of believers are of interest to the Christian educator and to the body of Christ. Consequently, this study is an examination of the Christian community's failure to effectively integrate the Christian faith in secular and Christian academic institutions. Without such an investigation the current secularization of our culture cannot be remedied. In an effort to promulgate Christianity and Judeo-Christian values in institutions across America and the world, this study will provide Christian educators with the tools necessary to effectively integrate prayer, Scripture, faith, forgiveness and redemption in their teaching practices and the lives of millions of minds and hearts around the globe. It is my hope that this text will provide parents, teachers, pastors, and Christian educators with a sound biblical understanding for embracing and communicating the cultural mandate (Genesis 1:28) and the Great Commission (Matthew 28:18-20) as they relate to the field of education. Presented in this manuscript are some hard truths about our current educational system and how Christians can make a difference in light of the cultural and moral decadence of our great nation.

The Subject

Everyone has a value set that determines his or her view of the world. However, a recent national survey of adults conducted by the Barna Research Group indicated that only 4 percent of adults have a biblical worldview as the basis of their decision making. The findings from this survey are astonishing, even more surprising is that the survey also discovered that only 9 percent of born again Christians have such a perspective on life.[1] Our perception of truth, and what we esteem the most, directly impacts how we judge every-thing around us. It also determines the level of influence we will have on others. Questions regarding theology, anthropology, philosophy, worldview, culture, religion, the integration of faith in education and their relationship to higher education and societal trends are but a few of the most current issues of concern for Christian educators.

Let me take a moment to address my fellow educators. Christian educators must always present an accurate view of God, of man, and of our world (the cosmos). We want our values to be biblically informed and reasonably developed. As Christian educators, it is our responsibility to teach our students to see their world through the lens of a Christian worldview. This is not a responsibility that should be taken lightly, as the Bible warns of the consequences if we fail to do so. The development of a Christian worldview through teaching and learning is of the utmost importance if one is to adhere to the warnings of Scripture. "My brethren, let not many of you become teachers, knowing that we shall receive a stricter judgment" (James 3:1). This work represents an attempt to provide a guideline to those already involved in the educational enterprise as well as to Christians who have a vision of becoming educators.

The Potential of the Study

It should be stated at the outset that such a study requires a thorough understanding of the subjects related to worldviews in higher education by tracing the history of the discipline. The subject is presented as an exploration of the various issues involved and provides an appreciation of the Christian heritage in the field of education by looking at the wider philosophical thought and theological fallout of Christian institutions. The historical roots and philosophical underpinnings of societal issues to current cultural trends are examined in light of the Christian community's failure to integrate and engage the culture. The purpose of this book is to provide the reader with more than just valuable insight regarding the past; the emphasis is on presenting proactive solutions for today that will result in a cultural reformation and transformation. The historical and scriptural analysis of religion in education is aimed at preparing Christians, particularly the Christian parent and Christian educator to be better equipped to serve society. After reading this text, the reader will be better prepared to meet the various challenges that await them in an anti-Christian and post-modern world. Toward this end, I will echo the words of the late Dr. Ronald Nash, "I am a Christian. As a Christian, I'm concerned about the future of the Christian Church, which rests to a large extent on the minds, hearts, and hands of its young people. Wrong choices about higher education have led many Christians to reject their faith. Many others have failed to reach their potential because the college they selected failed them in important respects."[2] It is the potential of education to instill secular worldviews that prompted the writing of this book, and it is the value of a Christ-centered education that demands a Christian worldview.

The Limitations of the Study

Spiritual development is foundational to academic pursuit for Christians. The Bible states that the fear of the Lord is the beginning of wisdom, and Christian Institutions (colleges, universities and seminaries) must put that truth into action through their choices of personnel, curriculum development and academic programs. In this post-Christian, post-modern society, people are declaring that there are no all-inclusive standards of morality, no unequivocal rules of behavior, no unchanging code of ethics, and that truth is relative, and not absolute. Such individualism touts the idea that religion, morals, and values are strictly personal choices and that the highest goal in life is one's own self-fulfillment, or to live for the moment. A proper worldview will renew the mind and shape the will, while bringing to bear the reality of the eternity we all face. This book is not intended to be an unabridged or complete treatment of the subject.

The Hope

The purpose of this study is to explore what the Bible says about teaching and learning (education), the role of Christians in education and the educational process. It is my hope that readers will gain some insight into the critical issues that must be addressed when envisioning the development of a Christian worldview. Issues to be discussed will include religion in academia and society, the humanism of higher education (Christian and secular institutions), the biblical mandate of Christian educators, the Christian educator's struggle in academic departments and suggestions for redeeming the Christian worldview through education.

This book is designed to examine the developmental process of spiritual formation through biblical, theological, educational, and religious training. The factors that influence the spiritual growth of believers are of interest to the Christian educator and to the body of Christ. Thus, *Christianity & Culture: a Christian Perspective on Worldview Development* is an examination of the Christian community's failure to effectively integrate the Christian faith in secular and academic institutions.

NOTES

[1] Barna Research Group, *A Biblical Worldview Has a Radical Effect on a Person's Life*. Ventura, CA: Barna Update (December 1, 2003). Retrieved on December 15, 2008 from http://www.barna.org/FlexPage.aspx?Page=BarnaUpdate&BarnaUpdateID=154.

[2] Ronald H. Nash, *The Christian Parent and Student Guide to Choosing a College*. (Brentwood, TN: Wolgemuth & Hyatt Publishers, 1989), 3.

Chapter 1

OVERVIEW OF RELIGION
IN SOCIETY

—⁓—

Historical Perspectives

Historically, religion has always played a major role in humanity's quest for the meaning and purpose of human existence. The great seventeenth century French mathematician, scientist, and Christian apologist Blaise Pascal (1623-1662) wrote in his *Pensées*, "What else does this craving, and this helplessness, proclaim but that there was once in man a true happiness, of which all that now remains is the empty print and trace? This he tries in vain to fill with everything around him, seeking in things that are not there the help he cannot find in those that are, though none can help, since this infinite abyss can be filled only with an infinite and immutable object; in other words by God himself."[1] Pascal's comments have often been translated to mean that "There is a God shaped vacuum in every man," which cannot be filled by any created thing, but God the Creator.

In many discussions of contemporary religion there is an implicit conception of social or cultural evolution; and the emergence of cultural ideals are often the result of various religious underpinnings. Human beings are spiritual beings who naturally seek to have religious or spiritual experiences. As a result, this human propensity to satisfy the deep longing to know the Creator has been manifested within the fabric of every culture.

According to Dr. Robert L. Simonds, professor and author at the University of California (San Diego) multicultural curriculum, "The United States of America has a multitude of religions, each with a unique culture of its own." Like many other aspects of culture, Simonds said that the religions of America are a melting pot that affects all parts of our society to some degree. In spite of this fact, Simonds argues that America still has one dominant culture: Evangelical Christianity as our country was founded upon the ideas and principles outlined in the Christian faith.

In proving his point, Dr. Simonds went on to emphatically make the following observations about America as a Christian nation[2]:

The Christian faith and its biblical principles, established in our Declaration of Independence and the U.S. Constitution, gave America and the world a completely new concept of government, one of allowing the church to be totally **FREE** of the dictates of the state (for the first time in history): in which the states (the body politic) were established for the protection of the free and independent church and its doctrine of *"Christian Self-Government with Union."* The Christian church was expected to raise up generations of men and women capable of maintaining the Constitutional principles of "self-government by union," the uniquely Christian and American ideal of civil government.

The American nation has a Constitution, established upon the biblical ***"Ten Commandments."*** The Bill of Rights was taken directly from the Biblical principles of Christianity. The central figure of both the Bible and of all Christendom is Jesus Christ. Jesus Christ re-established morality in its utmost purity. Jesus gave mankind and every individual the principles and rules to live by, to help every person be more perfect and fulfilled.

Christianity and its doctrines of love, service and liberty have long been established in America. Before Christianity had been applied to society, through civil government, the world only had government by autocracy (a single absolute ruler) as one extreme; and pure democracy (rule by the majority) at the opposite extreme. Both of these systems had major flaws. The influence of Christianity and the American forefather's belief in one God and Creator, established the first government in history as a REPUBLIC — a democratic republic. This Christian form of government became known as the "*golden mean*" between autocracy (kings and dictators) and pure democracy (majoritarianism, without regard to minority views).

Thus, Christianity, based upon the Bible, provided the basis for the first successful civil government that allows the civil rights of minorities, women's freedom, and religious freedom for all religions, free speech, free press, and free elections. Most of those liberties came directly from the Bible and Christianity.

Secular, Religious, and Legal Definitions

Religion, we have said, has been very present in the life of humans from the very genesis of culture. Religion is much more important to Americans than to people living in other wealthy nations. Six-in-ten (59%) of people in the U.S. say religion plays a very important role in their lives.[3] This data is based on a 2002 study conducted by the Pew Global Attitudes Project, in which the United States was the only developed nation whose inhabitants consider themselves as religious rather than secular.

Dr. Simonds in his work records that, "the culture of a people is made up of their religious structures, intellectual and artistic manifestations and long-lived traditions. Therefore, "*Cultural Relativity*" refers to cultural traits with all their complexities, which cannot be understood or evaluated without reference to the function in the broader culture as a whole. Prerequisite to "*tolerance*" and conciliation is an understanding of one another's culture."

The American culture has permeated throughout the *Christian culture of love, law, freedom, liberty and justice* for all. However, the American culture has been threatened and attacked by secularism.

In an unpublished doctoral dissertation project, Robert L. Waggoner said the following about the secularization of America.[4]

Generally speaking, a culture derived from biblical theism differs drastically from a culture derived from humanistic ideology. Those humanistic values have increased in the American culture and that theistic values have been diminishing may be illustrated in many ways, one of which is by observing historical changes in the United States over the past century. Since the family is a microcosm of the culture, then a brief overview at what has been happening to the family will illustrate changes in the culture in the United States. How humanism has overthrown theism in culture through education and law will then be observed.

The institution of the family has been assaulted drastically by humanistic ideology since World War II. Our former theistic morality has been replaced by humanistic immoralities of abortion, divorce and sexual permissiveness. Pornography and homosexuality also challenge Christian morality, while theistic family authority and economics are challenged by humanistic philosophies of materialism, feminism and statism.

America has become a pluralist society with many beliefs (political, religious, cultural and social) that must co-exist and participate together in society for the American culture and all other cultures to survive. Consequently, prejudice and religious discrimination must be prevented through education and understanding, that is a Christian doctrine, as well as a judicial mandate in American society. To accomplish such a difficult task one must be equipped with the secular, religious and legal terms associated with the cultural trends, especially the terms that relate to worldview development (See the Worldview Studies Glossary in Appendix C).

Christian Faith and Political Correctness

Don Closson, Education Research Associate for Probe Ministries, believes that the political correctness movement is sweeping institutions of higher learning worldwide. As stated by Closson, the term politically correct refers to the type of ethical and moral relativism that assumes that all cultures and systems of thought are equal in value.[5] While proponents of the politically correct movement argue that their goal is to propagate a philosophy of inclusion and multi-culturalism, what they have created in fact, is a movement meant to silence and stifle any views that do not fit into their own philosophy. More specifically however, these groups seek to silence conservative Christian ideas. Closson states:

> What those in authority on our campuses really hope to accomplish is the unquestioned implementation of a world-view that releases man from his moral obligation to a creator God, a God who sees all men and women regardless of their color, as in need of redemption. As Christian parents and alumni, we need to make certain that colleges remain places where students can seek and find the truth.[6]

Russ Wise of Christian Information Ministries agrees. According to Wise, humanism is the dominant view among educators in the United States. In fact, in his article, "Education and New Age Humanism" Wise quotes former National Education Association Honorary President and Humanist Manifesto co-signer, Charles Francis Potter as he shares his views about public school education, "Education is thus a most powerful ally of Humanism, and every American public school is a school of Humanism. "What," says Potter, "can the theistic Sunday Schools, meeting for an hour once a week, and teaching only a fraction of the children, do to stem the tide of a five-day program of humanistic teaching?"[7]

Wise states that these programs, which begin in grade school and continue through college, are designed to "free" pupils from Judeo-Christian backgrounds of the values and instruction that they receive from their parents and from the church. The result then is a system with "no basis of discerning right and wrong" and no absolutes.[8] Thus, those Christians in the United States and around the world who stand on biblical principles and who refuse to compromise their values even in the face of pressure from dominant culture face ridicule, persecution, and attack in higher education. This is ironic as many of the most highly regarded institutions of higher learning in our nation were founded in order to equip ministers for Christian service. Among these institutions are Ivy League universities such as Harvard, Yale, and Princeton. The history of these institutions and others, as well as the dynamics of education and religion, will be covered in depth in the next chapter.

NOTES

[1] Blaise Pascal. *Pensées*. Translated by A. J. Krailsheimer. (London: Penguin, 1966), #148, 75.

[2] Robert L. Sidmonds, *Religion and Culture in History: Teacher Guidelines for Teaching the Christian/ American Culture.* (San Diego, CA: A Unit in Multicultural Curriculum, The California History-Social Science Project at the University of California, n.d.). Retrieved on November 14, 2003 from http://www.nace-cee.org/teachingchculture.htm

[3] Robert L. Waggoner, *Biblical Theism vs. Secular Humanism: A Class to Train Theists to Confront Humanism.* (Brentwood, TN: Erskine Theological Seminary, 2000), 11.

[4] The Pew Research Center for the People and the Press. *The Pew Global Attitudes Project: U.S. Stands alone in its Embrace of Religion.* (Washington, D.C.: The Pew Research Center, 2002), 1. Retrieved on December 18, 2008 from http://pewglobal.org/reports/pdf/167.pdf.

[5] Don Closson, *Politically Correct Education.* (Richardson, TX: Probe Ministries, 1992), 1.

[6] Ibid., 4.

[7] Russ Wise, *Education and New Age Humanism.* (Richardson, TX: Probe Ministries, 1995), 2.

[8] Ibid., 2.

PART TWO

SPIRITUALITY, RELIGION

& WORLDVIEWS

IN ACADEMIA

Chapter 2

The Dynamics of Education

—ɷ—

"To prepare us for complete living is the function which education
has to discharge"
H. Spenser[1]

Philosophy of Education

Christian educators and stakeholders in education (parents,
teachers, pastors, churches and faith-based organisms) have
recently increased their scrutiny on the societal impact of higher
education (secular and Christian) on the culture at large. Stakeholders
generally want to know what students are getting out of their educational experiences, with a definite shift in emphasis from what is
being taught to what is being learned. This paradigm shift demands
a review of the philosophy of education and the values found in
every educational theory.

Philosophy, as we know it, is the path and passion to understanding the ultimate principles of the whole of reality. Its desire is
to explore ideas about God, about humanity, and about the universe
in which we live. Webster's Dictionary describes Education[2] as "the
profession of teaching. It is the act or process of learning as determined by the knowledge, skill, or discipline of character, acquired."

Thus, it is the act or process of training by a prescribed or customary course of study or discipline.

The word philosophy is made up of two words, "love" (*philo*) and "wisdom" (*sophia*), or the "love of wisdom." Thus, it is easy to comprehend how a great number of philosophers have devoted a great deal of study and prose to the subject of education. What is a philosophy of education? A philosophy of education recognizes that the enterprise of a civil society depends on the education of the young, and that to educate children as responsible, thoughtful and enterprising citizens is an intricate, challenging task requiring deep understanding of ethical principles, moral values, political theory, aesthetics, and economics; not to mention an understanding of who children are, in themselves and in society.

Key Terms in Philosophy[3]

Metaphysics: The branch of philosophy that deals with the nature of reality. In short, philosophers try to draw back the curtain of nonessentials of life to examine what remains.

Epistemology: The branch of philosophy concerned with the theory of knowing and of knowledge. It deals with the nature of learning. As such it is significant for teachers because it is closely affiliated with teaching methods and how students learn.

Axiology: is the area of philosophy concerned with value, and as such it is divided into two areas, **ethics**, and **aesthetics**. Ethics deals with moral values and appropriate conduct; aesthetics considers values in beauty and art. Educators have always addressed the need for students to engage in proper conduct and ethics.

Education as a social science has been influenced by five major philosophies that have contributed to our modern educational system. These include idealism, realism, pragmatism (known as progressivism), perennialism and existentialism. They reflect certain key voices in the philosophy of education, who have contributed in large part to our basic understandings of what education is and can be, and who have also provided powerful critical perspectives revealing the problems in education as it has been practiced in various historical circumstances.

Idealism

In education, idealism is a philosophy that is based on the view that reality is a world within a person's mind. As one of the oldest of the traditional philosophies, idealism goes back to Plato, who developed idealist principles in ancient Athens.[4] It is by definition, the philosophy that asserts that reality is spiritual in nature. Individuals must attempt to attain ideals or models of perfection. Idealism can also be described as "idea-ism," for instance, Plato's hierarchical view of reality, suggests that the forms or ideas are ultimately real and material objects as comprising a less real "copy" of the ideal world.

Realism

Realism, like idealism, is one of the oldest philosophical stances in the world. Realists believe that objects exist regardless of how we perceive them. Realism promotes the study of science–empirical, objective and experimental—with its precise measurements, and the scientific method. According to realism, there are essential ideas and facts to be learned through education; therefore lecture and other formal methods of teaching are useful.

Realism still influences education in many ways. A particular strategy used by a modern realist is to teach scientific reasoning, not facts. They may illustrate the reasoning with original accounts of famous experiments. This gives students a human side to the science and shows the reasoning in action. Most importantly, it shows the uncertainty and false steps of real science.

Educational Pragmatism/Progressivism

Pragmatism also known as progressivism is the belief that education must be based on the fact that humans are social animals who learn best in real-life activities with other people. Progressivists claimed to rely on the best available scientific theories of learning. Most believed that children learned as if they were scientists, following a process similar to John Dewey's scientific method and model of learning, and includes these steps:

1.   Become aware of the problem.
2.   Define the problem.
3.   Propose hypotheses to solve it.
4.   Evaluate the consequences of the hypotheses from one's past experience.
5.   Test the most likely solution.

Given this view of human nature, a progressivist teacher desires to provide not just reading and drill, but also real-world experiences and activities that center on the real life of students. A typical progressivist slogan is "Learn by Doing!"

George F. Kneller identified the major themes of this aforementioned theory or philosophy of education in chapter three of *Introduction to the Philosophy of Education*.

PROGRESSIVISM
(John Dewey, William H. Kilpatrick, John Childs)

1. Education should be life itself, not a preparation for living.
2. Learning should be directly related to the interests of the child.
3. Learning through problem solving should take precedence over the inculcating of subject matter, but maintain focus on subject matter.
4. The teacher's role is not to direct but to advise.
5. The school should encourage cooperation rather than competition.
6. Only democracy permits – indeed encourages – the free interplay of ideas and personalities that is a necessary condition of true growth.

Educational Perennialism[5]

The educational perennialists believe that the most important topics develop a person. Since details of fact change constantly, these cannot be the most important. Therefore, one should teach principles, not facts. Since people are human, one should teach first about humans, not machines or techniques. Since people are people first, and workers second if at all, one should teach liberal topics first, not vocational topics.

A Pennsylvania State University professor wrote the following about perennialism and those who hold the philosophy in education:

> For Perennialists, the aim of education is to ensure that students acquire understandings about the great ideas of Western civilization. These ideas have the potential for solving problems in any era. The focus is to teach ideas that are everlasting, to seek enduring truths which are constant, not changing, as the natural and human worlds at their most essential level, do not change. A Perennialist views nature, human nature, and the underlying principles of existence as constant. The principles of knowledge are enduring. Truth never changes.[6]

ESSENTIALISM (William Bagley, Herman Horne)

1. Learning, of its very nature, involves hard work and often-unwilling application.
2. The initiative in education should lie with the teacher rather than with the pupil.
3. The heart of the educational process is the assimilation of prescribed subject matter.
4. The school should retain traditional methods of mental discipline.

Although perennialism may seem similar to essentialism, perennialism focuses first on personal development, while essentialism focuses first on essential skills. Essentialist curricula, thus tends to be much more vocational and fact-based, and far less liberal and principle-based. Both philosophies are typically considered to be teacher-centered, as opposed to student-centered philosophies of education such as progressivism. However, since the teachers associated with perennialism are in one sense the authors of the Western masterpieces themselves, these teachers may be open to student criticism through the associated Socratic Method, which if carried out as true dialogue, is a balance between students, including the on-site teacher who is promoting the discussion.

The general objective of perennialism is to better prepare the learner for authentic education. According to Mortimer Adler, perennialism's objectives serve two categories of students. Adler makes this assertion:

> For those whose schooling ends after twelve years, that basic phase has prepared them for adult learning beyond all schooling. For others, it has prepared them not solely for adult learning but also for more schooling of an advanced kind, in the so-called institutions of higher education: colleges, universities, and technical schools.
> The education that takes place there is often called the higher learning. It would be more appropriate to it as further learning, for there is still more education to be had and further learning to be done, beyond the higher learning.
> Under whatever name, these higher institutions have been severely crippled by the inadequate preparation of those who successfully apply for entrance. The improvement of basic schooling, by which we seek to raise its quality for all, will also do much more than is to be desired. It will prepare and motivate more young people to go on to college, and this enlarged and better-prepared student body will enable our colleges to raise their sights and to become the centers of higher education that they profess to be.[7]

Mortimer Adler's contributions to the great conversation in philosophy, the great ideas of Western Civilization, and the philosophy of education have been the subject of various debates. Regardless of public opinion on authentic education, Adler's work in educational perennialism has led to a healthy debate on learning and values.

Educational Existentialism

Existentialism proposes that we should not accept any predetermined creed or philosophical system and from that try to define who we are. It aims for the progressing of humanity. Existentialists are in favor of independent thinking. Existentialism is not a set of curricular materials. Rather, it is a point of view that influences all that the teacher teaches and how he or she teaches. According to David E. Denton, Existentialism is a philosophy that warrants an accurate assessment of its influence in American educational philosophy. When discussing this concept in an article entitled, "Existentialism in American Educational Philosophy," Denton writes the following:

> Existentialism is an extremely popular topic among undergraduates on American college and university campuses. Students have become quite involved with the writings of such thinkers as Jean-Paul Sartre and Albert Camus. On almost any campus, one can start an immediate debate over the relative merits of these and other writers. This enthusiasm has spilled over into education courses, particularly those labeled philosophy of education and foundations of education. Professors, on more than one occasion, have been forced to "catch up" with their students by the insistent questioning of those students. Several texts in philosophy of education, by now including sections or chapters on existentialism, have given students additional opportunity to raise such questions. And a few universities, because of the orientations of the professors involved, actively encourage students in education to grapple with the topics and questions of existentialism.[8]

Existentialism engages the student in central questions of defining life and who we are and it attempts to help the student acknowledge his or her freedom and to accept the responsibility for that freedom. It also aims to help the student realize that the answers imposed from the outside may not be real answers. The only real answers are the ones that come from inside each person and are authentically his or her own.

Critique and Perspective[9]

The modern philosophies of pragmatism and existentialism, despite their differences, have several points in common. In contrast to traditional philosophies, both reject *a priori* (Latin, meaning "from what comes before," referring to deductive reasoning) epistemological considerations and downplay metaphysical ultimates and essences beyond the reach of humanity. In addition, both are relativistic in terms of values and truth, and both are humanistic or human-centered. A major difference between pragmatism and existentialism is that the former bases its relativism and humanism on the authority of society, while the latter stresses the role of the individual.

In education, the modern philosophies, in addition to the differences discussed in this section, also have likeness. For example, both see the teacher as being more of a guide or facilitator than an authority figure; both believe the curriculum should center in one way or another around the needs of the child or student, rather than around a solid core of unchanging "Truth"; and both reject the role of the school as primarily an institution for transmission of past knowledge to future generations.

Both existentialism and pragmatism have affected recent education. By far, the largest impact has been made by pragmatism. In fact, the pragmatic influence made an impression on every aspect of modern education – from architecture, moveable classroom furniture, and an activity center to a curriculum at all levels of education that has been broadened to include the practical and useful in addition to the academic. Many observers have noted that pragmatism has "transformed" schooling in the United States and other countries. The impact of existentialism has been more recent and, thus far, less dramatic. Certainly, however, the movements in alternative education, educational humanism, and de-schooling that arose in the 1970's found a major portion of their roots in existentialism. Both existentialism and pragmatism were having a renewed impact upon education in the 1990's through postmodernism. We will examine the impact of such philosophies in Chapter 6.

Other Influential Factors on Education

The educational field has been influenced by other powerful domains unrelated to the aforementioned philosophical stances, namely idealism, realism, pragmatism and existentialism. Educators who take their profession seriously pay attention to developments in other fields, such as psychology.

Constructivism

Constructivism, like existentialism, puts the learner at the center of the educational stage. Constructivism asserts that knowledge cannot be handed from one person to another (from a teacher to a learner), but must be constructed by each learner through interpreting and reinterpreting a constant flow of information. Thus, constructivism holds that knowledge is not transmitted unchanged from teacher to student, but instead that learning is an active process of recreating knowledge. Constructivists teach techniques that place emphasis on the role of learning activities in a good curriculum. Constructivists believe that people continually try to make sense and bring order to the world.[10]

Behaviorism

Behaviorism or behaviourism (not to be confused with behavioralism of political science) is an approach to psychology based on the proposition that behavior can be researched scientifically without recourse to inner mental states. It is a form of materialism, denying any independent significance for the mind. Its significance for psychological treatment has been profound, making it one of the pillars of pharmacological therapy.

One of the assumptions of behaviorist thought is that free will is illusory, and that all behavior is determined by a combination of forces comprised of genetic factors and the environment, either through association and/or through reinforcement.

The behaviorist school of thought ran concurrent with the psycho-analysis movement of 20th century psychology. Its main influences were Ivan Pavlov, who investigated classical conditioning, John B. Watson (1878-1958) who rejected introspective methods and sought to restrict psychology to experimental methods, and B. F. Skinner, who sought to give ethical ground to behaviorism, relating it to pragmatism. We will explore this philosophy more closely when we discuss the psychology of education.

We have looked at four major philosophies and two psycho-logical factors that most 21st century educators and parents need to become familiar with because of their influence on education. They are very much a part of our current system of education at every level and are viewed as being a reality.

The basis of all the educational systems of the ages is formed in a foundational philosophy. The philosophies of the Greeks, the Romans, the British, and Americans still speak throughout the centuries. Sad to say, some Christian educators, their schools and other Christian organizations are polluted with the philosophy, curriculum, methodology, and productivity of the world's secular, humanistic, and progressive education. I will discuss this thought further in the chapter entitled Principal Factors (Religious Stands & Philosophical views section).

It is the power of philosophical teachings that has shaped nations, governments, and movements. If philosophy is powerful, then Christians must recognize and evaluate it. In contrast, the philosophy of Christian Education is grounded in the Word of God. In Jeremiah 10:2a (KJV) we read, "Learn not the way of the heathen (or the unsaved)..." Not that we should not know their ways, but that we do not embrace their basic tenets. In Colossians 2:8, Paul also tells us to, "Beware lest any man spoil you through philos-ophy and vain deceit, after the tradition of men, after the rudiments of the world, and not after Christ." Unfortunately, our generation has not taken heed to this warning, because many Christians, both young and old, are learning and copying the ways of the world. They have become rebellious. Parents are not honored. Interest in morality, holiness and in genuine spiritual life (a Christ-like life) is declining. Consequently, lawlessness is becoming more prevalent. It was John Dewey (1859-1952), the American philosopher, psychologist, and educational reformer whose thought has been greatly influential in the United States and around the world. Dewey's philosophy of education[11] and the teachers college at Columbia University in New York became the flame from which the torches of other teachers' colleges around the country were lit. Dewey's anti faith, pragmatic, progressive educational philosophy has swept the nation's school systems.

The divine antidotes for these social dilemmas are found in the Scriptures, where we find the core of Christian teachings. For instance, Psalms 119:11 (King James Version) states, "Thy Word have I hid in my heart, that I might not sin against thee." And Proverbs 19:27 (New King James Version) gives this command: "Cease listening to instruction, my son, and you will stray from the words of knowledge." Do our children receive teaching that turns them from God's truth? If yes, the Christian philosophy of education calls for an educational process that puts the Bible at the center, and that asks the student and the teacher (or parent) to evaluate all they see in the world through the eyes of God. This is the mandate for every Christian educator because God will demand an account for every seed planted in the mind of students (*see* James 3:1).[12]

Christian Education

"Today we have a weakness in our educational process in failing to understand the natural associations between the disciplines. We tend to study all our disciplines in unrelated parallel lines. This tends to be true in both Christian and secular education. This is one of the reasons why evangelical Christians have been taken by surprise at the tremendous shift that has come in our generation."
- Francis A. Schaeffer[13]

Christian Education and Old Testament Scriptures

The history of Christian education in America and the world cannot be studied apart from the historical heritage provided by the Hebrew educational system and the early church, for Christianity finds its roots in Judaism. Early Christians for the most part accepted and read the Hebrew scriptures, particularly those books—such as Genesis, Exodus, Numbers, Leviticus, Deuteronomy, Isaiah, the Psalms, and the Song of Songs—that they saw as foreshadowing the events of Christianity. However, it is in the book of Deuteronomy that we trace the roots of Christian Education. In Deuteronomy 6:4-9, Moses uttered the commandments, statutes, and judgments that the Lord God had commanded him to teach. These were the very words of Moses:

> 4 "Hear, O Israel: The LORD our God, the LORD *is* one! 5 You shall love the LORD your God with all your heart, with all your soul, and with all your strength. 6 "And these words which I command you today shall be in your heart. 7 You shall teach them diligently to your children, and shall talk of them when you sit in your house, when you walk by the way, when you lie down, and when you rise up. 8 You shall bind them as a sign on your hand, and they shall be as frontlets between your eyes. 9 You shall write them on the doorposts of your house and on your gates. [14]

The words of Moses to the children of Israel came after a recital of the Ten Commandments originally given in Exodus 20:2-17 (see Deut. 5:1-21). Though Hebrew education as we know it began with Abraham and the covenant, it was not until the time of Moses that it became national and personal with profound implications.

Christian Education professors, Dr. Kenneth O. Gangel and Dr. Warren S. Benson maintained that Christian Education is rooted in the Hebrew Educational system of Deuteronomy by saying the following about its historical significance:

It (Deuteronomy 6:4-9) was a contract between the Hebrews and God, but also between each individual Hebrew and God. Every person in the nation had an individual obligation to God, to his family, and his nation.

But how was that obligation to be communicated? How was it to be maintained as the nomadic families and tribes of the patriarchs wandered across the sun-baked plains of the land we now call Israel? Perhaps it survived because that most crucial of all educational elements—aim, or objective— was never distorted or diminished in the minds of Hebrew parents. Theirs was the task of training the next generation, and failure in that task would not be taken lightly by the God who had called them to it.[15]

Herein, we find the principle outlined in Proverbs 22:6, where we are instructed to "train up a child in the way he should go, and when he is old he will not depart from it." It is within this context that the Christian educator is to educate the next generation. We must teach every discipline within the framework of Judeo-Christian values. It is still the general aim of education, to develop productive citizens who will contribute to society.

Christian Education and New Testament Scriptures

The first thing to notice about the early Church is that its members had an urgent message for a civilization that already contained the seeds of its own demise. Early Christianity was, above all, a missionary enterprise, an evangelical movement in a world ripe for its teachings. At the end of His public life, Christ commanded His disciples, to "Go into all the world and preach the gospel to every creature." (Mark 16:15). In addition to the journeys recorded in the New Testament, historically, the gospel was spread all over the world through the apostolic teachings of the Christian faith. Thus, the New Testament concept of Christian education began with the evangelization of the world and the teachings of the early church. The overall theme within New Testament writings is to know Christ; the intermediate goal is to educate through discipleship; and the cultural outcome is to equip believers to serve Christ and others. It was Gangel and Benson, who said, "Making disciples was the central imperative among going, baptizing, and teaching of all nations, which were descriptive of what is involved in the making of disciples."[16] The concept of discipleship is outlined in Colossians 2:1, 5-8, where Paul wrote:

"I want you to know what conflict I have for you.... for though I am absent in the flesh, yet I am with you in spirit, rejoicing to see your good order and the steadfastness of your faith in Christ. As you therefore have received Christ, so walk in Him, rooted and built up in Him and established in the faith, as you have been taught, abounding in it with thanksgiving. Beware lest anyone cheat you through philosophy and empty deceit, according to the basic principles of the world, and not according to Christ."

Paul, out of concern for the believers at Colossae, warned them concerning the worldly philosophies that the ungodly teach; teachings that demote Christ with the intent that the basic principles of Christianity be denied. Consequently, Paul encouraged the early church to develop a comprehensive biblical worldview that would enable them to understand and engage culture in a respectful and constructive manner.

The Place of Christian Education in Church History

Paul's warnings have been echoed throughout the various ages of church history: From the Apostolic Age with the apostles Paul, Peter and John to the early Church Fathers with Clement of Rome, Ignatius, and Polycarp, the apologists defended the faith against enemies both within and outside the Church. Men of renown like Justin Martyr, Irenaeus, and Origen proved to be effective in their battle against the false teachings and philosophies of their day, including Gnosticism. Giants like Athanasius and Augustine dominated the history of Christian philosophy and solidified the theology of Christianity. Christianity faced some fierce opposition in every age; from the Medieval Church to the Reformation Age which resulted in the nailing of Martin Luther's Ninety-Five Theses for debate on the Castle Church door at Wittenberg. Though the battle remained the same, Christianity's archenemies have certainly changed their strategy by waging war on worldviews within the legal and educational front.

The battle to win the minds of children, adolescents, and university students is what is at stake in the cultural war being waged in the public square. In essence, early Christians presented a reasoned statement or a verbal defense of Christian belief through their teachings. John B. Hulst rightly summarized this perspective when he said, "It is the purpose of our educational, academic activity to seek to understand and transmit an understanding of creation and its history. This is so that kingdom citizens may understand the creation and their place in it and their calling to bring to expression the kingdom rule of Jesus Christ over all things."[17]

The Founding of American Education

Spiritual Formation: Historical Perspective

"Religion has been banished from the public square (except in times of national crisis) and exiled to reservation ruled by faith. Faith is viewed as a subjective, emotive quality leaned upon by the weak or uneducated. It is the opiate of the masses, the bromide for the unintelligent. Faith is a crutch to support the psychologically crippled—those who lack the scientific and sophisticated view of the real world." R.C. Sproul[18]

Education has played a major role in the spiritual formation of individuals for centuries. Historically, schools have had the responsibility of passing on a society's culture to the younger generation. In a very real sense, today's citizens are living tributes to past investments and ideas of yesterday's educators. The sociological influence of education (both secular and religious) on the lives of its recipients should never be underestimated.

One may think that schools in America were established to teach children the three Rs of 'reading', 'writing', and 'arithmetic'; in actuality the fear of God helped establish our public school system as well as higher education. No authentic history of spiritual formation within the American system of education can be written without a brief review of the rich heritage inherited from the Pilgrims and Puritans. Myra Pollack Sadker, and David Miller Sadker pointedly said the following concerning the role of religion in education: "The religious fervor that drove the Puritans to America also drove them to provide religious education for the young, making New England the cradle of American education."[19] Highlighting the role of education in American colonies, authors Stephen Tchudi and Diana Mitchell echo the following sentiments: "When the colonists fled from England to the New World and inscribed the date of 1642 on Plymouth Rock, their possessions included this long tradition of interest in literacy and models of instruction. By 1648, the colonists in Massachusetts demonstrated their interest in education by passing a law that every community of more than fifty families must provide instruction in the 3Rs of reading, writing, and arithmetic."[20]

The New England Primer introduced colonial children to their ABC's by means of pictures and rhymes such as these.

In Adam's fall
We sinned all.

Thy life to mend,
This Book attend.

The Cat doth play,
And after slay.

A Dog will bite
A thief at night.

An Eagle s flight
Is out of sight

The idle Fool
Is whipt at school.

As runs the Glass,
Man's life doth pass.

My Book and Heart
Shall never part.

Job feels the rod,
And blesses God.

Proud Korah's troops
Were swallowed up.

The Lion bold
The lamb doth hold.

The Moon shines bright
In time of night.

Figure 1: The New England Primer was first published by Benjamin Harris, an English bookseller and writer of anti-Catholic verses who from 1686 to 1695 lived in Boston, Massachusetts. This Figure was retrieved from *en.wikipedia.org/wiki/New_England_Primer*

Our choice for a starting point, then, of literacy instruction in America, is the little poem shown. It is one of the earliest efforts to motivate students to learn by extolling the virtues of literacy and learning. Tchudi and Mitchell went on to say the following:

"The instructional strategy — the "pedagogy" — of the *Primer* went back over two thousand years to the pattern followed by the Greeks. The Alphabet was taught and retaught with a variety of poems and mnemonic devices: A— "In Adam's Fall/We sinned all", F—The idle *Fool*/Is whip't at School." (The latter suggests that instructional methodology might not have changed much from the Greeks either; literacy learning was seen as a rote skill requiring considerable discipline, and if that discipline were not forthcoming spontaneously from the young scholar, it would be administered by the teacher.)"

Commenting on New England's educational history and the Puritans, Gangel and Benson made the following observations; "The educational interests of Puritan education stemmed from its understanding of the nature of man. Because man is inherently evil and fallen, he must be taught the Bible in order to be brought to a realization of his depravity and to be led to repentance."[21] They were convinced that "only supernatural grace could overcome total depravity, but the ability to love and keep God's law indicated that a person was a child of God."[22]

In an attempt to gain momentum in their effort to promulgate their fundamental Christian beliefs, they created a system of education where instruction often began at home (Dame Schools). Later developments led to the passing of laws such as the **Old Deluder Satan Law**, aimed at making education a social responsibility through the establishment of a feeding program for higher education and at making progress in their stated mission to save souls. According to higher education historian, John R. Thelin:

If one looks at the colonies associated with the founding of Harvard, Yale, and Princeton, it is evident that college-building was serious business. Congregationalists and Presbyterians—what might be collectively described as Puritans—had definite ideas about collegiate education as part of a large, important social, religious, and political vision. As a group, Puritans had tended to be dissenters in matters of religion.[23]

The Puritans established various institutions of higher learning; many of the colleges and universities began as small, religiously sponsored institutions founded to train the clergy. The first fifteen institutions of higher education established in the colonies were all affiliated with a religious denomination.

The Development of Colonial Higher Education[24]
Table 1

Year	Institution	Year	Institution
1636	Harvard University	1769	Dartmouth University
1693	College of William & Mary	1782	Washington College
1701	Yale College	1782	Washington and Lee University
1746	Princeton University	1783	Hampton-Sidney College
1754	King's College (Columbia University)	1783	Transylvania College
1755	University of Pennsylvania	1783	Dickinson College
1764	Brown University	1784	St. John's College
1766	Queen's College (Rutgers University)		

Literature on the history of the American university within a religious perspective can provide a legitimate contribution to the highest level of scholarship on higher education and its role in society. John H. Roberts and James Turner, outlined the ties between American higher education, religion, and the sciences in their book, *The Sacred and Secular University*, when they wrote:

Prior to 1870, colleges typically functioned as the intellectual arm of American protestantism. Indeed, the Protestant churches had given birth to higher education in North America and had nurtured it for much of its history. Even institutions created under the auspices of the states, though typically nonsectarian and willing to leave the finer points of theology to denominational seminaries, nevertheless remained, in the words of the University of Michigan president Henry P. Tappan, "under the protecting nurturing wing of Christianity." As late as 1868 Illinois Industrial University (later the University of Illinois) included in its official inaugural ceremonies hymns, scriptural passages, and prayers. Its first president, John Gregory, lost few opportunities to emphasize his university's Christian Character.

Although colleges were often founded to train ministers, few institutions of higher education limited their student body to ministerial candidates. The central vocation of colleges for most of the nineteenth century was promoting the development of Christian civilization through the education of learned "gentlemen." The close association between religion and higher education became most visible in the extra-curricular aspects of student life – in the establishment of compulsory chapel and the promotion of periodic revivals of religion on campus. In the academic realm the role of religion was slightly refracted by the colleges' commitment to imbue students with what the widely circulated Yale Report of 1828 termed *"the discipline...of the mind."* This commitment reflected the reign of faculty psychology, which conceived of the mind as a set of powers, or "faculties," that could be trained and even strengthened with appropriate exercises. In practice, commitment to disciplining the mind meant that colleges generally devoted their first two years to mathematics and classics. Thereafter they focused more on providing students with *"furniture of the mind"* by offering them a more diverse curriculum predicated on the assumption that nature and society alike could best be understood through the prism of Christian theology.[25]

Clearly then, higher education's earliest role in society was to promote and propagate Christian values and, in so doing, aid in developing a Christian civilization. Sadly, one would never know this by looking at many of the first fifteen institutions of higher learning today. Now bent on secular humanism and anti-Christian values, many of these institutions reject and attack the virtues upon which they were built.

What religious artifacts, if any, still exist on these campuses today?

A closer look into the origins of the aforementioned elite colleges and universities (as known today), will prove that they were founded as religious institutions with a curriculum intentionally designed to integrate faith and learning. For instance, Harvard College's website (now Harvard University), provides evidence for the purpose of its founding. The following can be found in the archive of Harvard University's Graduate School of Arts and Sciences, Christian Fellowship page.[26]

About our shield and logo

1. Harvard University was founded in 1636 with the intention of establishing a school to train Christian ministers. In accordance with that vision, Harvard's "Rules and Precepts," adopted in 1646, stated (original spelling and Scriptural references retained):

2. Let every Student be plainly instructed, and earnestly pressed to consider well, the maine end of his life and studies is, to know God and Jesus Christ which is eternal life (John 17:3) and therefore to lay Christ in the bottome, as the only foundation of all sound knowledge and Learning. And seeing the Lord only giveth wisdom, Let every one seriously set himself by prayer in secret to seeketh it of him (Prov. 2:3).

3. Every one shall so exercise himself in reading the Scriptures twice a day, that he shall be ready to give such an account of his proficiency therein, both in Theoretical observations of Language and Logic, and in practical and spiritual truths, as his Tutor shall require, according to his ability; seeing the entrance of the word giveth light, it giveth understanding to the simple (Psalm 119:130)." The motto of the University adopted in 1692 was **"Veritas Christo et Ecclesiae"** which translated from Latin means **"Truth for Christ and the Church."** This phrase was embedded on a shield as shown

to the right, and can be found on many buildings around campus including the Widener library, Memorial Church, and various dorms in Harvard Yard.

Interestingly, the top two books on the shield are face up while the bottom book is face down. This symbolizes the limits of reason, and the need for God's revelation.

Consistent with "Veritas Christo et Ecclesiae" and the purpose of Harvard's founding, our fellowship is dedicated to discovering and experiencing Truth (Veritas) for the sake of Christ and his church.

Gangel and Benson (1983) wrote the following concerning the Puritans' commitment to education and the preservation of their faith.[27]

Though the early Puritans shared a commitment to education in the home, the close ties between church and state made government involvement in New England education inevitable. As early as 1636, the Massachusetts General Court appropriated 400 pounds toward the founding of a school to teach and train students for Christian Ministry—

Harvard College. In fact the first three American colleges, Harvard (1636), William and Mary (1693), and Yale (1701), were opened because of religious motivations. Yale was begun because Harvard was softening its stance on Calvinist doctrines.

History indicates that while schools existed in colonial America, they were generally private and considered to be extensions of the home; they were not funded by government taxes, except in Massachusetts.[28]

For the first two hundred years in American history, from the mid-1600s to the mid-1800s, public schools as we know them were virtually non-existent.... In these two centuries, America produced several generations of highly skilled and literate men and women who laid the foundation for a nation dedicated to the principles of freedom and self-government... The private system of education in which our forefathers were educated included home, school, church, voluntary associations such as library companies and philosophical societies.... The Bible was the single most important cultural influence in the lives of Anglo-Americans. Thus, the cornerstone of early American education was the belief that "children are an heritage of the Lord." As our forefathers searched their Bibles, they found that the function of government was to protect life and property. Education was not the responsibility of the civil government.[29]

Since the education of children was assumed to be the responsibility of parents, rather than that of civil government, education was not compulsory but supported by family and philanthropic funds. The fact that the overarching belief was that "children are a heritage from the Lord" proved the Puritans' commitment to integrate religion (faith) with learning. This is evident in established educational enterprises as early as the home schooling system known as the Dames Schools, the passing of the Old Deluder Satan Law, and the founding of the Boston Latin Grammar School which led to the creation of American High School. The Sadkers commented on that era by stating, "Within a year of the founding of the Boston Latin Grammar School, Harvard College was established specifically to prepare ministers. Founded in 1636, Harvard was the first college in America, the jewel in the Puritans' religious and educational crown."[30] This view of education and religion not only made higher education useful for vocation, but vital for spiritual formation. In thinking of the founding of American higher education and its institutions; one cannot afford to overlook their religious heritage in light of the current secularization of these institutions and their progressive fall into what is now viewed as postmodernism.

NOTES

[1] Webster's Revised Unabridged Dictionary (1913), 471.

[2] Ibid., 471.

[3] Pamela J. Farris. *Teaching and Bearing the Torch.* (Boston, MA: Mc Graw-Hill College, 1999), 88-93.

[4] Allan C. Ornstein and Daniel U. Levine. *Foundations of Education.* (Boston: Houghton Mifflin Company, 2000), 392.

[5] Richard D. Mosier, *"Perennialism in Education,"* History of Education Journal 2, no. 3 (Spring, 1951): 80-85.

[6] Pennsylvania State University. Retrieved on May 23, 2008 from "http://www2.yk.psu.edu/~jlg18/506/Word%20files/philosophy/Perennialism_reading.doc."

[7] Mortimer J. Adler, *The Paideia Proposal: An Educational Manifesto.* (New York, NY: Mcmillan Publishing Company, 1982), 69-70.

[8] David E. Denton, "Existentialism in American Educational Philosophy," *International Review of Education/ International Zeitschrift fürErziehungswissenschaft/ Revue Internationale de l'Éducation,* 14, No.1 , (1968):100-101. Retrieved on May 20, 2007 from http://www.jstor.org/stable/pdfplus/3442112.pdf

[9] Taken from George R. Knight. *Philosophy & Education: an Introduction in Christian Education.* (Berrien Springs, MI: Andrews University Press, 1998), 79.

[10] Myra Pollack Sadker and David Miller Sadker, *Teachers, Schools, and Society* (New York, NY: McGraw Hill Higher Education, 2005), 345.

[11] Internet Encyclopedia of Philosophy, University of Tennessee at Martin Retrieved on May 7, 2008 from "http://www.iep.utm.edu/d/dewey.htm" University of Tennessee at Martin, Dec 28, 2005.

[12] "My brethren, let not many of you become teachers, knowing that we shall receive a stricter judgment."

[13] Francis A. Schaffer, *Escape from Reason.* (Downers Grove, IL: Intervarsity Press, 2006 (originally printed in 1968), 17.

[14]These verses have been known in Jewish tradition for centuries as "The Shema," which contains the fundamental truth of Israel's religion. They are recited as a daily prayer along with Deuteronomy 11:13-21 and Numbers 15:37-41.

[15] Kenneth O. Gangel and Warren S. Benson, *Christian Education: Its History and Philosophy.* (Chicago, IL: Moody Press, 1983), 22.

[16] Ibid., 22.

[17] John B. Huslt, "Key Note Address" Christian Worldview and Scholarship, ed. John B. Hulst (Melbourne, Australia: Amani, 2004), 16.

[18] R.C. Sproul, *Defending Your Faith: An Introduction to Apologetics.* (Wheaton, IL: Crossway Publishing, 2003), 7.

[19] Myra Pollack Sadker and David Miller Sadker, *Teachers, Schools, and Society* (New York, NY: McGraw Hill Higher Education, 2005), 285.

[20] Stephen Tchudi and Diana Mitchell, *Exploring and Teaching the English Language Arts* (Reading, MA: Addison Wesley Educational Publishers, Inc., 1999), 5.

[21] Kenneth O. Gangel and Warren S. Benson, *Christian Education: Its History and Philosophy*. (Chicago, IL: Moody Press, 1983), 230.

[22] Ibid., 230.

[23] John R. Thelin, *A History of American Higher Education*. (Baltimore, MD: The John Hopkins University Press, 2004), 23.

[24] Myra Pollack Sadker and David Miller Sadker, *Teachers, Schools, and Society* (New York, NY: McGraw-Hill Higher Education), 289.

[25] John H. Roberts and James Turner, *The Sacred and the Secular University* (Princeton: Princeton University Press, 2000), 20.

[26] Harvard University, About the shield and Logo of Harvard University. Retrieved December 24, 2005, from http://hcs.harvard.edu/~gsascf/shield.html

[27] Kenneth O. Gangel and Warren S. Benson, *Christian Education: Its History and Philosophy*. (Chicago, IL: Moody Press, 1983), 232.

[28] "The general principle in the matter of public education is that anyone is free to found a public school and to direct it as he pleases. It's an industry like other industries, the consumers being the judges and the state taking no hand whatever... There has never been under the sun person as enlightened as the population of the north of the United States." Alexis De Tocqueville, quoted in George W. Pierson (1959). *Tocqueville in America*. (Garden City: Anchor Books), 293-294. "Apart from New England, where tax-supported schools existed under state law, the United States, from 1789 to 1835, had a completely *lassés-faire* system of education.... there were no compulsory attendance laws anywhere. Parents educated their children as they wished.... There was no need for any child to go without an education. The rate of literacy in the United States

then was probably higher than it is today." Samuel L. Blumenfield (1985). *Is Public Education Necessary?* (Boise, Idaho: The Paradigm Company), 27.

[29] Robert A. Peterson (1979). *Education in Colonial America.* Cited by Rus Walton (1987). *One Nation Under God.* (Nashville: Thomas Nelson Publishers), 61.

[30] Myra Pollack Sadker and David Miller Sadker, *Teachers, Schools, and Society* (New York, NY: McGraw-Hill Higher Education), 289.

Chapter 3

The Dynamics of Religion

—ɯ—

Philosophy of Religion: a common worldview

As mentioned in chapter 2, the word philosophy comes from the ancient Greek word " $\phi \iota \lambda o \sigma o \phi \iota \alpha$ " (philosophos) or the Latin *philosophia*, which means "love of wisdom." The discipline of philosophy once included all forms of knowledge and all methods for attaining it. Early scientists, regardless of their field of study, called themselves "natural philosophers." But through the rise of universities and the separation of learning disciplines, philosophy has taken on more specialized meanings. Not all philosophers agree on what the word 'philosophy' means, variously contending amongst the following views of philosophy:

a. A *method* of rational inquiry, with the approaches used varying considerably. For instance, the Socratic Method relies primarily upon asking questions while analytic philosophy applies logic and language in other ways.

b. A particular *subject matter*. The scope of philosophical inquiry is diverse, and includes methaphysics, epistemology, ethics, and logic.

c.   A *process*. Goals of this process include providing an antidote to certain confusions of language, as Ludwig Wittgenstein, the famous Austrian philosopher once proposed.

d.   An academic *discipline*, studied at universities and colleges worldwide.

e.   The term can also refer to a worldview, to a perspective on an issue, or to the position of a particular philosopher or school of philosophy. Popularly, it may also refer to a person's perspective on life (as in "philosophy of life") or the basic principles behind, or method of achieving, something (as in "my philosophy about driving on highways").

The phrase "a philosophical attitude" refers to a thoughtful approach to life. Reacting to a tragedy *philosophically* might mean abstaining from passionate reactions in favor of intellectual detachment. This usage arose from the example of Socrates, who calmly discussed the nature of the soul with his followers before drinking a deadly potion of hemlock as ordered by an Athenian jury. The Stoics followed Socrates in seeking freedom from their passions, hence the modern use of the term *stoic* to refer to calm fortitude. While many are very intrigued by the study of philosophy, it is often closely related to other studies like history, science and religion. Religion is perhaps one of the most engaging of all the disciplines associated with philosophy. A working definition of the word religion is sometimes used interchangeably with faith or belief system —and is commonly defined as belief concerning the supernatural, sacred, or divine; and the moral codes, practices, values, institutions and rituals associated with such belief. In its broadest sense some have defined it as the sum total of answers given to explain humankind's relationship with the universe. In the course of its development, it has taken many forms in various cultures and individuals. In fact, no culture is deprived of a worldview or of a philosophy. As C.S. Lewis asserted, everyone in life has a philosophy – the only question is, whether it is a good one. He said, "Good philosophy must exist, if for no other reason, because of bad philosophy."[1] Moreover, this raises the question: Is there such a thing as the philosophy of religion? The answer is an emphatic, yes! It is defined in metaphysics as the "the study of the nature of reality, of what exists in the world, what it is like, and how it is ordered," particularly about the nature and existence of God (or gods, or the divine).[2]

The philosophy of religion is at the core of every religious experience whether good or bad. Josh McDowell and Don Stewart (1992) have described religion as "that aspect of one's experience in which he attempts to live harmoniously with the power or powers he believes are controlling the world."[3] Thus, every religion presumably carries her own philosophy. The question remains, however whether non-Christian religions may be said in any way to represent a "saving structure which serves to point to the cosmic Christ."[4]

What role does the philosophy of religion play in the life of the Christian? R.C. Sproul (1986) writes, "No society can survive, no civilization can function without some unifying system of thought.... What makes a society a unified system? Some kind of glue is found in a unifying system of thought, what we call a worldview."[5] The fact of the matter is that thoughts shape societies. And there is no better place to shape the thoughts and views of this generation on religion than in the classrooms of America. Therefore, it is incumbent upon us to see that worldviews, or philosophies whether secular or religious, are important. Christians, then, need to study philosophy. Stressing this point, Ronald Nash (1988) writes the following:

> Because so many elements of a worldview are philosophical in nature, Christians need to become more conscious of the importance of philosophy. Though philosophy and religion [i.e., theology] often use language and often [wrongly] arrive at different conclusions; they deal with the same questions, which include questions about what exists (metaphysics), how humans should live (ethics), and how human beings know (epistemology). Philosophy matters. It matters because the Christian worldview has an intrinsic connection to philosophy, and the world of ideas. It matters because philosophy is related in a critically important way to life, culture,

and religion. And it matters because the systems opposing Christianity use philosophical methods and arguments.[6]

As we have seen in the writings of R.C. Sproul and Ronald Nash, all metaphysical, ethical, and epistemological principles points of view are assumed by and incorporated in religion, and it is the business of the philosophy of religion to understand and rationally evaluate them. At the end of our journey here on earth will we end our quest for a philosophy of religion with the words of Friedrich Nietzsche who said that "God is dead" or will we echo the words of Immanuel Kant who said that "It is morally necessary to assume the existence of God."

In Colossians 2:6-8, the Apostle Paul tells us to walk in Christ just as we, "have received Christ Jesus the Lord, so walk in Him, rooted and built in Him and established in the faith, as you have been taught, abounding in it with thanksgiving. Beware lest anyone cheat you through philosophy and empty deceit according to the tradition of men, according to the basic principles of the world, and not according to Christ."

Essentially the study of philosophy and religion are very much a part of education, particularly higher education. Therefore, it is incumbent upon the Christian to be actively involved in presenting an authentic, evangelical view in philosophy and religion. The Christian worldview must permeate our philosophical framework.

Psychology of Religion

We have already explored the philosophy of religion as it relates to education. Now we will address the psychology of religion as consistent with the educational enterprise. Certainly, anyone interested in the history of the world and the antecedents of his culture will find the study of religious psychology an imperative. It is an activity that is found in every society and culture throughout human history. American society is no different from any other society; it too has its wealth in religious thought, particularly religion and educational psychology.

The term religion has its origin in the Latin *religere*, which means to bind fast, to moor, or to unite. One question we face as educators is this: how should we examine the psychology of religion in education, particularly higher education? Are values perceived or created? The role of society in the shaping of values, with contributions from sociological and psychological theories, is a critical study in the area of religious influence. No institutions have influenced society more than the family (Marriage), religion (Church), and education (Schools) with educational institutions having the greatest access to the human mind statistically. Individuals spend more hours learning over the course of a lifetime in academic settings than anywhere else. The learning process takes place at various levels such as through parents, religious leaders (mostly a few hours a week), literature (books, newspapers etc...) the media (radio, television), and most of all in the classroom where most people learn to assimilate in their respective culture. Educators, particularly Christian educators regardless of where they teach, should never underestimate the power that they have in shaping the minds of a nation. We are told to "Train up a child in the way he should go, and when he is old he will not depart from it" (Proverbs 22:6). This does not mean that we Christianize our teaching in the public schools but it implies that we must speak truth with nothing crooked (Proverbs 8:6-8). Any introduction to the classical theories in the psychology of religion would lead us to various psychologists like William James, Sigmund Freud, and John Dewey; All of whom have influenced the direction of American education as well as the psycho-social and educational theories such as role theory, motivations, attribution, and sociobiology-evolutionary psychology. In parallel, as educators we must clarify psychological frameworks of teaching and the bonds of the psychology of religion to related domains such as spirituality, morality and ethics. Finally, we must thrust ourselves by asking the methodological questions specifically related to the psychology of religion.

William James

William James, an American psychologist and philosopher who served as president of the American Psychological Association, wrote

Varieties of Religious Experience. In this book, James proposed that because there are so many different definitions of the word religion, we should learn that the whole concept is too large for any one definition to fit all. Instead, religion should be seen as a collective name. James wrote that religion, in the broadest sense, "consists of the belief that there is an unseen order, and that our supreme good lies in harmoniously adjusting ourselves thereto."[7] He distinguished between institutional religion and personal religion. Institutional religion refers to the religious group or organization, and plays an important part in a society's culture. Personal religion, in which the individual has a mystical experience, can be experienced regardless of the culture (James, 1902). James was most interested in understanding personal religious experiences.

If personal religious experiences were what James preferred, dogmatism was something that he disliked. Dogmatic thought, whether religious or scientific, was anathema to James. The importance of James to the psychology of religion—and to psychology more generally—is difficult to overstate. He discussed many essential issues that remain of vital concern today. Authors Bruce Bickel and Stan Jants (2002) said that, "Every single person thinks about God. Now, he or she may picture God as –

- an impersonal force that infuses every part of the universe,
- a spirit that inhabits every person like a kind divine light,
- a powerful Creator who made the universe and then took a long vacation, never to return,
- a personal spirit being who made the universe and then stayed very involved, or
- something that doesn't exist at all.

But in one way or another everyone has a God idea."[8]

Sigmund Freud

Throughout his life, Psychologist Sigmund Freud sought to answer many of life's questions with his ideas and theories of psychoanalysis. Many of the questions that picqued Freud's interest had to do with the complexities of the human soul and the ways in which various factors manifest themselves in human behavior; one such question was, "Why are people religious?"

Religion was, for Freud, nothing but psychology projected into the external world. When writing about the source of religion, Freud expressed that religious needs derive from human beings' sense of vulnerability or "the infant's helplessness and longing for the father."[9] According to Freud, religion, biologically speaking, is to be traced back to the small child's long, drawn-out helplessness. This longing for the Father, inevitably constitutes the root of every form of religion, and calls up the entanglement of the Oedipus complex,[10] including feelings of fear and guilt. Though Freud was right in his assumption that there is a sense of vulnerability within every human being, his conclusion was wrong. Man's sense of helplessness is not based on a "longing for the father" but on the depravity of man, the sinful nature. Freud's psychology of religion is certainly an effort to deny the existence of God.

Sigmund Freud is the father of psychoanalysis. Freud believed that personality has these three structures: the *id*, the *ego*, and the *superego*. The *id* has the quality of being unconscious and contains everything that is inherited, everything that is present at birth, and the instincts (Freud). The *ego* has the quality of being conscious and is responsible for controlling the demands of the id and the external world. In addition, the ego responds to stimulation by either adaptation or flight, regulates activity, and strives to achieve pleasure and avoid displeasure. Finally, the superego, whose demands are managed by the id, is responsible for the limitation of satisfactions and represents the influence of others such as parents, teachers, and role models, as well as the impact of racial, societal, cultural and religious traditions.

In *Moses and Monotheism* (1939), Freud reconstructed biblical history in accord with his general theory, but biblical scholars and historians would not accept his account since it was in opposition to the point of view of the accepted criteria of historical evidence. His ideas were also developed in *The Future of an Illusion* (1927). When Freud spoke of religion as an illusion, he maintained that it is a fantasy structure from which a man must be set free if he is to grow to maturity; and in his treatment of the unconscious he moved toward atheism. Unlike Freud's religious and scientific skepticism, Christianity views its biblical truths as exclusive, the knowledge of the Christ. In *Can Man live without God?*, Dr. Ravi Zacharias expressed his disagreement with those who voice Freud's sentiments toward religion.[11]

> Christianity is often scorned as the pariah among the religions of the world and considered by its detractors to be controversial because modern learning mocks the very notion of truth as absolute. The Christian faith is often castigated because the contemporary mind-set is infuriated by any claim to ideational elitism in a pluralistic society. How dare one idea be claimed as superior to another? After all, we are supposed to be a multicultural society: should no truth also come in different dress?

Influenced by the interplay of biological neurosis and atheism, Freud's views created presuppositions that led to secular and humanistic worldviews of religion. Freud's skepticism reveals a set of beliefs that falls beyond the scope of empirical sciences to offer a definitive verdict on the truth or falsity of religion as an ontological worldview. Dr. R. C. Sproul answered the question of religion, when he made the following observation, "Freud and others could not deny that religious belief is virtually universal. Indeed religion is so prevalent on the planet that we can say of man that he is not only *homo sapiens*; he is also *homo religiosus*."[12]

John Dewey

John Dewey, one of America's most influential progressive educators, viewed education as a social process seeking social ends. Though Dewey has been dead nearly half a century, his educational thoughts are very much alive and have permeated the philosophy of education in America. Therefore, it is the Christian educators' responsibility to become familiar with his philosophy and to be equipped with a biblical perspective on Dewey's controversial interpretations of anthropology, personal dynamics and agnostic beliefs.

Raised in a Christian home in Vermont prior to the Civil war, John Dewey's childhood was filled with biblical teaching and the memorization of Scripture. Dewey recalls that the religion of his childhood "centered about sin and being good" and on the love of Jesus Christ "as Savior from sin."[13] Perhaps, Dewey's mother, a committed Christian, pushed young Dewey to become a follower of Jesus Christ too intensely because as he grew older, he developed a very naturalistic approach to life. Despite his Christian upbringing, Dewey developed a worldview that was heavily influenced by Darwinian teaching. Over time, Dewey grew very distant from the Christian faith and adopted more democratic values. He sought to incorporate the methods of scientific inquiry with both academic and democratic ideals. As a critical naturalist, Dewey accepted natural knowledge as the total of everything; therefore, the Divine Being was not responsible for creation.[14]

Dewey's Education

In the early 19th century, "a new faith in the social sciences and social planning gained a foothold"[15] in American education. The American educational system experienced a drastic shift when it changed from a teacher-centered to a student-centered approach to learning. John Dewey was the chief proponent of this new era in American educational progressivism.

Christians (ministers, parents, educators and students) must thoroughly review Dewey's academic background and those who influenced his life, if and when we desire to develop a proper under-standing of his philosophy of education. In *A Christian Perspective on John Dewey*, Dr. Werner Lumm wrote the following regarding the significant influences in Dewey's background[16]:

While Dewey was an undergraduate student at the University of Vermont, Matthew Buckman, the president of the university, taught him to "think for himself" rather than to accept the beliefs of others. After he graduated, H. A. P. Torrey, his former professor of philosophy, encouraged him to pursue philosophy as a career. While he was a graduate student in philosophy at John Hopkins University, his thinking was heavily influenced by the following three men: (a) George Sylvester Morris, who had religious orthodoxy of his own "puritanic New England upbringing" and who was secularizing philosophy, a heretofore theological subject, as quickly as he could; (b) G. Stanley Hall, who due to growing skepticism had abandoned theological studies for philosophy and literature, who had developed a psychological system structured within an evolutionary framework, and who was strongly advocating child-centered education; and (c) Charles Sanders Peirce generally recognized as the founder of pragmatism, who placed strong emphasis on scientific methodology.

As seen in his professional career, Dewey addressed a range of issues and areas in philosophy, but all in relation to human life and educational activity. He was interested in the progress of the sciences, and his concerns combined a background of naturalism, progressivism, and instrumentalism or functionalism. Author Robert W. Pazmiño[17] made an interesting observation concerning the pedagogy of John Dewey when he said; "Dewey sought to synthesize child-centered and content-centered approaches in education. He also sought to combine emphases on the school and society in the hope that the school would become a microcosm of the society."[18]

The Role of Doctrine in Religious Education

The commitment, sustained effort, and creativity of educators will be crucial to improving the teaching and learning process. Teachers, administrators, Christian educators and parents will have to consider carefully and work out curricular and instructional approaches to achieving excellence in education. The instructional approaches used by these stakeholders must include a career-oriented preparation that embraces a Christian worldview of life through sound application of Biblical doctrines of all academic subjects.

The education of the young is primarily the role of parents, the church and, of course, of the educational authorities in society that include academic institutions at all levels including administrators, teachers and those who train educators in schools, colleges, and universities.

Responsibility of the Family

The primary role players in a child's education, parents, are responsible for rearing the next generation of children in the fear of the LORD. They must support their children by taking heed to the scriptural mandate to be God-fearing examples by not forsaking the assembling of the saints and by teaching and receiving a godly education.

When discussing the effect of higher education on religious faith, in a chapter on the same subject, the late Dr. Ronald Nash wrote the following, "Parents and students need to understand that there is something about the educational process itself that serves to weaken and undermine the values that students may bring to their college experience."[19] Dr. Nash went on to quote James Hunter, a sociologist at the University of Virginia who wrote:

> Somehow exposure to the realm of higher education weakened the grip of religious conviction over a person's life. Thus whatever religious beliefs and practices an individual carried with him at the start of his educational sojourn would have been either seriously compromised or abandoned altogether by the time he was ready to graduate. Minimally holding on to the religion of his adolescence would have proven difficult if not impossible.[20]

God's principles of accountability must first be taught in the home. We must instill these values into our children's lives. These principles include the worship of God (our human purpose), man's depravity (sin), God's means of salvation (the new birth) as well as the biblical mandates to do business until Christ comes (Luke 19:13).

The Church

The Church proclaims biblical doctrines and truth, which form the theological foundation for the family. Doctrine and truth encourage and guide parents, from scripture, to take up their biblical responsibility to educate and to raise their children in the fear of the LORD. Craig R. Dykstra in his essay, *No Longer Strangers: the Church and its Educational Ministry*, addressed the subject of "Christian education for participation in redemptive activity" by writing the following on the issue:

> Christian education is that particular work which the Church does to teach the historical, communal, difficult, countercultural practices of the Church so that the Church may learn to participate in them ever more fully and deeply. It is the dialogical process of teaching and learning through which the Church comes to see, grasp and participate ever more deeply in the redemptive transformation of personal and social life that God is carrying out.
>
> There is no possibility of a Christian education where there is no Church, where there is no body of believers, fellow citizens with the saints and members of the household of God being built into the redemptive work of God in Christ Jesus. But because, in Christ, a people have been called and have responded and still today are called and do respond (however imperfectly and perhaps even halfheartedly), we too may join in, participating in life. And because of all that, we can do Christian education.[21]

At the heart of Christianity is the teaching of faith (relationship with God); Jesus Christ is referred to as "Teacher" (John 3:2), the Holy Spirit's ministry includes teaching (John 14:26) and the Great Commission includes "teaching them to observe all things I have commanded you" (Matthew 28:20). Christianity and the Church have always supported education.

The Schools

The school expounds on the biblical worldview, looking at all areas of life from mathematics, to the sciences, to the languages and the arts from a biblical, Christian perspective. This is to equip the Christian student to take dominion for Christ and His Kingdom. It is an extension of the parent's mandate to "train up a child in the way he should go [according to his character, calling and God-given talents]" (Proverbs 22:6) and the Church's mandate to "make disciples of all nations" (Matthew 28:19).

Dr. John A. Hughes, professor of education at the Master's College, outlined the purpose and goal of education in an essay entitled, *Why Christian Education and not Secular Indoctrination.*[22] He wrote the following;

> Education gains purpose and significance to the extent it is consistent with and contributes toward accomplishment of God's highest purpose for man. Succinctly summarizing the teaching in scriptural passages such as Psalms 73:24-26, John 17:22-24, Romans 11:36, and I Corinthians 10:31, the Westminster Shorter Catechism states that "man's chief end is to glorify God and to enjoy Him forever." The highest goal of education must then be to assist individuals in developing the knowledge, skills, and attitudes that will enable them to better glorify and enjoy God.

The concept of teaching as a Christian educator is one that must embrace the developmental process of spiritual formation through biblical, theological, educational, and religious training. The overall character of education in the Judeo-Christian mind is to renew the mind and thus draw the heart of man to his Creator God.

All three institutions (family, church, and schools) are key role-players to support and reinforce each other and thus eliminate the erroneous secular humanist messages taught in the public school. Together, all three establishments foster godly discipline and, consequently, diminish criminal delinquency and strengthen

Christ-like character. Greater academic achievements are spawned as a result of godly discipline thus, it is imperative for parents to have a voice in the educational process in order to ensure account-ability. All three are subject to the Word of God. Moreover, we cannot underestimate the fact that our responsibility as Christian educators is to transmit the Word of God so that every student may be transformed by God's grace.

Conceptualizing the Instructional Process

The importance of the instructional aims (goals, objectives) in the teaching- learning process is seen in the functions they perform. An aim is a clear statement of what the educator hopes to accomplish by teaching the lesson. Instructional aims are valuable for planning, teaching, and evaluating of course content. In order to gain a better understanding of knowledge and the instructional process, it is necessary that the scholar-teacher understand how learning occurs. The instructor must understand how to conceptualize the process. How is this to be done?

Alfred North Whitehead provides the answer to this question.[23] According to Decker Walker and Jonas Soltis, authors of *Curriculum and Aims*:

> Whitehead chastised the schools for teaching students in a way that produced "inert knowledge": knowledge that connected or reacted with nothing in their lives and had little meaning for them. He argued that knowledge had to be mean-ingfully introduced and thoroughly learned and reflected on by students, rather than collected in encyclopedic fashion. His conception of the rhythm of education can be read as a corrective to such an encyclopedic view of educating and can be applied to the teaching of a subject, of a unit, of a lesson, and even to the elementary, secondary, and post-secondary articulation of education at large.

Walker and Soltis explain that Whitehead used the terms "Romance," "precision," and "generalization"- in order to characterize *the rhythm of education*, in which he shares his theory on the progression of a student in a formal learning situation.[24] In the text, Whitehead contends that one should begin an engagement with any subject in a passionate or romantic way. In other words, the student should be genuinely interested and intrigued by the subject matter. Whitehead also states, that "Getting to know the subject better and studying it in detail is what the stage of precision is all about." He believes that, "The passionate interest remains and becomes the driving force of self-discipline required for the hard work of studying the subject in detail." In fact, Whitehead is of the opinion that careful and thorough examination of a part is the essential ingredient to being able to achieve mastery of the whole. It is then, he says, that "generalization becomes possible and that some of the same passion present at the beginning of instruction remains towards the end." In this instance confidence in knowledge of the subject can be achieved because one understands it so well.

Whitehead's approach to educational mastery is of value to all students regardless of the subject matter or vocation that one strives to learn or master. As mentioned in greater detail earlier, "Whitehead sees the need for the rhythmic cycle of passion, precision, and generalization to repeat itself throughout the educational process." Contrary to the psychological methods and approaches proposed by other researchers and scholars, Whitehead's philosophy aims at producing students who are not only competent in a subject but who are passionate as well. Authors Walker and Soltis of *Curriculum and Aims* suggest another way of viewing Whitehead's educational theory.

NOTES

[1] C.S. Lewis, "hearing in War-time," *In the Weight of Glory* (San Francisco: HarperSanFrancisco, 1980), 59.

[2] Florida State University, *"What is Philosophy?"* Retrieved May 7, 2007 from "http://www.fsu.edu/~philo/new%20site/sub_category/whatisphilo.htm" What is philosophy?

[3] Josh McDowell and Don Stewart, *Handbook of Today's Religions* (Nashville, TN: Thomas Nelson Reference, 1992), 11.

[4] From Sir Norman Anderson, ed., *The World's Religions*, Grand Rapids, MI: William B. Eerdmans Publishing Company, 1976.

[5] R.C. Sproul, *Lifeviews* (Old Tappan H. Revell, 1986), 29.

[6] Ronald H. Nash, *Faith & Reason* (Grand Rapids, 1988), 26.

[7] William James (1902), *The Varieties of Religious Experience.* (New York: Longman), p. 53.

[8] Bruce Bickel and Stan Jantz, World *Religions and Cults 101: A Guide to Spiritual beliefs.* (Eugene, Oregon: Harvest House Publishers, 2002), p. 7.

[9] Sigmund Freud, *Civilization and its Discontent*, trans ed. James Strachey (New York: W.W. Norton, 1961), 19.

[10] In psychoanalysis, a subconscious sexual desire in a child, esp. a male child, for the parent of the opposite sex, this may result in neurosis in adulthood.

[11] Ravi Zacharias, *Can Man Live without God.* (Nashville, TN: Word Publishing Group, a Division of Thomas Nelson, 1994), 121.

[12] R.C. Sproul, *Defending your Faith: An Introduction to Apologetics.* (Wheaton, IL: Crossway Books, 2003), 158.

[13] Stephen C. Rockeffeler, *John Dewey: Religious Faith and Democratic Humanism* (New York: Columbia University Press, 1991), pp. 171-72.

[14] David H. Roper, *"John Dewey: A History of Religious Education,* ed. Elmer L. Towns (Grand Rapids: Baker Book House, 1975), 315.

[15] Michael J. Anthony, *Introducing Christian Education: Foundations for the Twenty-First Century,* (Grand Rapids, MI: Baker Academic, 2001), 30.

[16] Article based on Dr. Lumm's doctoral dissertation, reprinted from *Balance,* a publication of the School of Education, Bob Jones University.

L. Werner Lumm, *A Biblical Analysis of the Educational Philosophy expressed by John Dewey in his Original Writings.* Unpublished Dissertation, (Greenville, SC: Bob Jones University, 1996).

[17] Robert W. Pazmiño, *Foundational Issues in Christian Education* (Grand Rapids, MI: Baker Book House Company, 1997), 155.

[18] The best introduction to Dewey's educational thought is provided in Martin S. Dworkin, *Dewey on Education: Selections with an Introduction and Notes* (New York: Teachers College Press, 1959).

From a Christian perspective, Dewey must first be criticized for his ahistorical pragmaticism and presentism. Christianity is a historical faith. Second, Dewey must be criticized for his anti-super-natural bias that discounts the place of revelation. Christianity is revealed faith (religion). Third, Dewey must be criticized for his faith in progress and education and for his assumption that education can result in the salvation of persons. Christianity maintains the reality of sin and that salvation comes through faith in Jesus Christ by the grace of God. Beyond these criticisms, much can gained from a study of Dewey.

[19] Ronald H. Nash, *The Christian Parent and Student Guide to choosing a College* (Brentwood, TN: Wolgemuth & Hyatt, 1989), 90.

[20] James Davison Hunter, *Evangelicalism, The Coming Generation* (Chicago: University of Chicago Press, 1987), 172.

[21] Jeff Astley, Leslie J Francis and Colin Crowder (editors), *Theological Perspectives on Christian Formation: A Reader on Theology and Christian Education*, (Grand Rapids, MI: W. B. Eerdmans Publishing Company, 1996), 117.

[22] John MacArthur (General Editor) with the Master's College Faculty, *Think Biblically! Recovering a Christian Worldview*, (Wheaton, IL: Crossway Books, 2003), 245.

[23] Alfred North Whitehead, *The Rhythm of Education, The Aims of Education* and Other Essays. (New York, NY: The Free Press, 1967), chapter 2.

[24] Decker F. Walker, and Jonas F. Soltis, *Curriculum and Aims*. (New York, NY: Teachers College Press, 1986), 34-35.

Chapter 4

The Educator, the Mind and the Texts

—m—

Nearly three hundred years ago our universities were Christian, now they are secular and humanistic, what has gone wrong? We have failed to refute secular thinking; in part, this is due to the modern tendency to denigrate thinking as non-spiritual. However, there is a big battle going on to win the hearts and minds of people. We need bright Christians who are able to publicly refute the errors of modern thought and philosophy. We need to plan for the long term and encourage those who are intellectually gifted to enter our universities and institutions, and to enter the worldview debate. People are waiting for sound arguments to believe in God.

The Educator and the Scripture

We are to be salt and light to the world (Matthew 5:13-16). Salt both preserves and prevents decay. It also adds flavor. Edmund Burke (1729-1797) once said, "The only necessity for the triumph of evil is that good people do nothing" – passivity in the midst of evil is sin. The Apostle James tells us in his epistle, "Therefore, to him who knows to do good and does not do it, to him it is sin" (James 4:17).

In his essay *The Religious Life of Theological Students*, author Benjamin B. Warfield wrote the following on the subject of vocation[1]:

'Vocation'—it is the call of God, addressed to every man, whoever he may be, to lay upon him a particular work, no matter what. And the calls, and therefore also the called, stand on a complete equality with one another. The burgomaster is God's burgomaster; the physician is God's physician; the merchant is God's merchant; the laborer is God's laborer. Every vocation, liberal, as we call it, or manual, the humblest and the vilest in appearance as truly as the noblest and the most glorious, is of divine right."

Benjamin B. Warfield emphasized the God-given responsibility of the theological student, but the same responsibility is dually given to the religious educator. The apostle James eloquently expressed this responsibility when he penned, "My brethren, let not many of you become teachers, knowing that we shall receive a stricter judgment" (James 3:1). Thus, teachers are responsible not only for themselves but for all those they influence. Moreover, let us also remind ourselves that "All authority in heaven and on *earth*" has been given to Christ not to the devil (Matthew 28:18). While the mandate of the Great Commission is to make disciples; we are still to plunder the kingdom of Satan to bring freedom to those who suffer from spiritual or intellectual blindness, and 'open their eyes, and to turn them from darkness to light' (Acts 26:18). We can see from Paul that he debated, reasoned, persuaded, and defended the gospel in order to accomplish this purpose (Acts 9:29, 17:2, 17:17, 18:4, 18:19). How can this mandate be fulfilled save that we study to show ourselves approved unto God as "a worker who does not need to be ashamed" (II Timothy 2:15), by continually renewing our minds with the Scriptures (Romans 12:1-2) in order that Christ might be fully presented in our educational endeavors (Colossians 3:16-17). Thus, we must allow the four-fold purpose of the Scriptures to be seen through our profession as educators[2]: "All Scripture is given by inspiration of God, and is profitable for doctrine (teaching), for reproof (to convince), for correction (to make right), for instruction in righteousness (training in discipline toward righteousness), that the man of God may be complete, thoroughly equipped for every good work" (II Timothy 3:16-17).

Secular Worldview vs. Christian Worldview

The issue of worldviews in education is one of great concern for the 21st Century educational community. It is particularly important to the Christian community, for we are in the world but are not of this world (John 17:16). Education has the power to shape our views of God, the nature of man, and thought patterns of the mind in matters of faith, morality and ethics.

In our early discussion on the founding of the American system of higher education, I discussed the Christian heritage of various colleges and universities in America. This rich history is one where God is seen as Creator and man as a created being that is accountable to a loving God.

Dr. Ronald Nash (1936-2006), in his article *The Myth of a Value-Free Education* made the following statement, "Our educational crisis is to some extent a closing of the American mind, as Allan Bloom examined in his best selling book of that title. But it is more profound, a closing of the American heart. No real progress towards improving American education can occur until all of us realize that an education that ignores moral and religious beliefs cannot qualify as a quality education."[3] Similarly, Stanley Hauerwas in his essay, *The Gesture of a Truthful Story*, echoed the same sentiment on the role of religious education that produces a Christian Worldview:

> Put very simply religious education is the training in those gestures through which we learn the story of God and God's will for our lives. Religious education is not, therefore, something that is done to make us Christians, or something done after we have become Christian. Rather, it is ongoing training in the skills we need in order to live faithful to the Kingdom that has been initiated in Jesus. That Kingdom is constituted by a story that one never possesses, but rather constantly challenges us to be what we are but have not yet become.
> The primary task of being educated religiously or better Christianly, is not the achievement of better understanding but faithfulness.…..What we are asked to be is first and foremost a people who embody and manifest the habits of peace

characteristic of a forgiven people, not just those who provide worldviews through which to make sense of the world.[4]

In our day and age no one can deny the fact that our public education system has deteriorated greatly. In his book *Can Man Live without God*, best selling author Dr. Ravi Zacharias attributed this deterioration to our society's departure from God and His law. According to Zacharias, how you answer the questions of God's existence will impact your relationship with others, your commitment to integrity, your attitude toward morality, and your perception of truth.

The unregenerate man (non-Christian), of course, would give up anything rather than his cherished independence from God. Dr. Nash in the article *The Myth of a Value-Free Education* later wrote:

> College students today are surrounded by an allegedly academic setting in which the things they find most obvious are confusion, conflicting claims and the absence of any fixed points of reference. America's colleges have become centers of intellectual disorder. As David Gress explains, "Instead of being havens of independent thought, universities have become channels of indoctrination…confirming the prejudices of those who control the agenda of public discourse." Ralph Bennett is surely right when he warns that "behind its ivy-colored camouflage, American higher education is a fraud—untrue to its students, untrue to itself."
> The inadequacies of contemporary education are not exclusively matters of the mind. Traditional religious and moral values are under assault at every level of public and higher education. Our educational system is engaged in a systematic undermining of these values.[5]

The Christian Educator's Struggle in Academia and Religion Departments

The recent surge of antagonism on Judeo-Christian values in western culture can be credited by the increasing hostility toward theistic teachings. The crisis in American education is a direct result of man's attempt to remove God from the classroom and the world of academia all together. Only a few centuries ago, almost all state universities held compulsory chapel services, and some required Sunday church attendance as well. Today, however, the once pervasive influence of religion (Christianity) in the intellectual and cultural life of America's preeminent colleges and universities has all but vanished.[6]

The misconception of the *Separation of Church and State* has been the catalyst for the current animosity toward Christianity in the American educational and legal structure. The adaptation of various ill will concepts of freedom led to materialism, agnosticism and pluralistic views of truth, reality, and morality. In his book, *A Christian Manifesto*, Dr. Francis A. Schaeffer (1912-1984), wrote about the inception of our current cultural shift from Protestantism to pluralism or non-belief:

> Until recently it meant that the Christianity flowing from the reformation is not now as dominant in the country and in society as it was in the early days of the nation. After about 1848 the great influx of immigrants to the United States meant a sharp increase in viewpoints not shaped by Reformation Christianity. This, of course, is the situation which exists today. Thus as we stand for religious freedom today, we need to realize that this must include a general religious freedom from the control of the state for all religion. It will not mean just freedom for those who are Christians. It is then up to Christians to show that Christianity is the Truth of total reality in the open marketplace of freedom.
>
> This greater mixture in the United States, however, is now used as an excuse for the new meaning and connotation of pluralism. It now is used to mean that all types of situations are spread out before us, and that it really is up to each individual to grab one or the other on the way past, according to the whim of personal preference. What you take is only a matter of personal preference. Pluralism has come to mean that everything is acceptable. This new concept of pluralism

suddenly is everywhere. There is no right or wrong; it is just a matter of your personal preference.[7]

Dr. Schaeffer's analysis of the American culture was penned nearly a quarter century ago and spoke prophetically on the responsibility of Christians to engage our culture. Like many others who proclaim the importance of embodying a Christian worldview in every realm of society, Dr. Schaeffer expressed his hope for a cultural revolution in government, law and all of life whereby Christians would 'reestablish our Judeo-Christian foundation and turn the tide of moral decadence and loss of freedom.' No other place could this revolution have its most critical impact than in the educational system.

NOTES

[1] Benjamin B. Warfield, *The Religious Life of Theological Student*, (Phillipsburg, NJ: P & R Publishing, 1992), 4.

[2] This four-fold purpose I specifically outline in the biblical text to be teaching, to bring conviction, to make correction and to train the hearers to live a righteous life: a purpose that James later outlined in his epistle when he said that we ought to "be doers of the Word, and not hearers only, deceiving ourselves." (James 1:22)

[3] Ronald Nash, *The Myth of a value-Free Education*, (Grand Rapids, MI: Acton Institute, 2004), 1. Source: http://www.acton.org/publicat/randl/article.php?id=18

[4] Jeff Astley, Leslie J Francis and Colin Crowder (editors), *Theological Perspectives on Christian Formation: A Reader on Theology and Christian Education*, (Grand Rapids, MI: W. B. Eerdmans Publishing Company, 1996), 103.

[5] Ibid., 1.

[6] Back cover of George M. Marsden's book, *The Soul of the American University: from Protestant Establishment to Established Nonbelief* (Oxford, UK: Oxford University Press, 1994).

[7] Francis A. Schaffer, *A Christian Manifesto*. (Wheaton, IL: Crossway Books, 1981), 46-47.

PART THREE

THE ROLE

OF WORLDVIEW

FORMATION

IN

THE CURRICULUM

CHAPTER 5

RESEARCH DESIGN (AIM)

—ɯ—

"Our progress as a nation is no swifter than our progress
in education"
John Fitzgerald Kennedy

Overview of the Research Design

As noted in the acknowledgment, the ideas in this book are based primarily on research conducted on the subject of religion and worldviews in higher education. The study was designed primarily as a qualitative research (with some quantifiable data) based on my own conviction on the importance of bringing spiritual perspective to the field of education by challenging educators to consider the possibility of integrating faith, morality, Judeo-Christian values and the Christian worldview in the higher education classroom. In essence, the research initially was conducted to learn how worldviews are shaped at the university level and to learn how Christians can reclaim the grounds lost in the battle for the mind and hearts of this generation.

The review of the literature was conducted from an interdisciplinary array of sources for this topic. As the field of worldview research is an interdisciplinary one, sources consulted included those from the emerging literature in the field of close relationships; as well as cultural anthropology, apologetics, Christianity, faith, higher education, literature, philosophy, science, religion, spirituality, scripture (the Bible), theology and worldview issues (particularly those studies related to worldviews in higher education environments). Francis A. Schaeffer best described society's problem when he wrote:

> The basic problem of Christians in this country...in regard to society and in regard to government is that they have seen things in bits and pieces instead of totals. They have very gradually become disturbed over permissiveness, pornography, the public schools, the breakdown of the family, and finally abortion. But they have not seen this as a totality— each thing being a part, a symptom, of a much larger problem. They have failed to see that all of this has come about due to a shift in worldview—that is, through a fundamental change in the overall way people think and view the world and life as a whole. This shift has been away from a worldview that was at least vaguely Christian in people's memory toward something completely different...[1]

Undoubtedly, the current cultural emphasis on tolerance, pluralism, atheism and academic freedom provided a theoretical framework for review of essential pieces of research related to the structure, processes, and psychosocial results of worldviews in education.

Design and Method

The design and method of this text is aimed at providing an educational response to the academic impact of secularism in education. The philosophical influences of intellectualism are explored within the confines of various worldviews in higher education. Secondly, an examination of various spiritual issues related to the current secularization of institutions that were once Christian, as well as the lack of Christian influence within academic departments. Third, included is an analysis of the struggles that believers encounter within the college or university campus, both as students and faculty members. Finally, the emphasis is on providing practical ways to use the power of teaching to empower students to become inquisitive about the Christian view of life and to cultivate a sense of curiosity that ignites a passion for sound wisdom in contemporary issues.

Purpose and Objectives

This section of the book is specifically designed to examine the developmental process of spiritual formation through biblical, theological, educational, and religious training. The factors that influence the spiritual growth of believers are of interest to the Christian educator and to the body of Christ. Consequently, this study is an assessment of the Christian community's failure to effectively integrate the Christian faith into academic institutions and society as a whole. This section was written to provide Christian educators with the tools necessary to effectively integrate prayer, scripture, faith, forgiveness, and redemption into current teaching practices and into the lives of millions of minds worldwide.

In order to accomplish the outcomes of the research presented in this book, information from various academic, religious, public and private institutions of higher learning were collected. Research methods such as analytical surveys (academic and spiritual), as well as a qualitative, and systematic research in areas such as philosophy, theology, and religion in higher education proved to be essential.

NOTES

[1] Francis A. Schaffer, *A Christian Manifesto*. (Wheaton, IL: Crossway Books, 1981), 17-18.

CHAPTER 6

CURRICULUM DESIGN

—ᴍ—

Education without values, as useful as it is,
seems rather to make man a more clever devil.
C.S. Lewis

The field of education is guided by its curriculum and instruction. Curriculum is generally defined as the planned experiences provided through instruction that enable schools to meet their goals and objectives. The curriculum of a school reflects the values, beliefs, and mores of the local community, as do the textbooks selected for adoption and the books purchased for the school library.[1] According to Ornstein and Levine (2000), the organization of a curriculum is often viewed within two approaches, namely between the subject matter vs. student needs.[2] The aforementioned authors wrote the following concerning the issue of curriculum:

The various types of curriculum organization in American schools can be viewed from two perspectives. One emphasizes the subject to be taught; the other emphasizes the student. In the first case, the curriculum is seen as a body of content, or subject matter, that leads to certain achievement outcomes or products. The second approach defines curriculum in terms of the needs and attitudes of the student;

the concern is with process – in other words, how the student learns and the climate of the classroom or school.

Actually, the two views represent the extremes of a continuum, and most practitioners (and researchers) rely on some curriculum blend within this continuum. Few schools employ pure subject-centered (cognitive) or pure student-centered (psychological) approaches in the teaching-learning process. Even though most teachers tend to emphasize one approach over the other, they incorporate both choices in the classroom.

A well-designed curriculum can help students, regardless of their academic level, to acquire authentic knowledge of the subject matter, to learn skills, and to enhance their ability to perform in various life contexts (for example, at home, at work, and in society at large). The primary goal of teaching at the college level is to provide students with professional education that will enhance their service to the global community including the community of faith (the Christian Church). Other key goals include the acquisition of knowledge, the honing of one's ability to think critically, and the opportunity to become familiar with a particular area of inquiry. Curriculum development and instructional material design play an integral role in all levels of education whether at the elementary, middle, high school, or adult higher education level such as college, graduate school, and professional and theological education. Any education professional who is involved in the development of courses and instructional materials, the planning and grading of courses, the development of educational products, and the administration of educational programs at various levels particularly in higher education would do well to understand the role of curriculum design in the development of worldviews in society. In the words of famous eighteenth century British writer and lexicographer Samuel Johnson, "The supreme end of education is expert discernment in all things - the power to tell the good from the bad, the genuine from the counterfeit, and to prefer the good and the genuine to the bad and the counterfeit." Johnson

(1709-1784) once said, "in order that all men may be taught to speak truth, it is necessary that all should likewise hear it."

It is incumbent upon educators (particularly those of Christian conviction) to view higher education the way that our forerunners saw it: as a means of preparing men and women for works of service. Due to changes in human thinking brought on by modernist and postmodernist philosophy, a shift has taken place in most of the institutions of higher learning whose premises were to educate and train individuals for service. As a result, they have contributed to an increasingly humanistic and pluralistic society that is flooded by secular worldviews.

The early history of the American university proves that the general aim of its founders was to educate a learned clergy and a core of cultured and pious leaders who would dedicate themselves to public service.[3] Moreover, the field of education, including Christian higher education, has lost its theological moorings and has attempted to place its anchor in the shifting sands of the social sciences.[4] The current academic trend to abandon the traditional values of our forefathers is particularly seen in the content of academic curricula of all major fields of study. It is increasingly evident that we are living in "perilous times" (II Timothy 3:1-9), where the Christian faith and its truth are in conflict with the secular worldview of the current age of unbelief (I Timothy 4:1-2). If one is to make a difference in our world, he or she must grasp these profoundly contrary views of reality, for they are the roots of our cultural crisis. According to Colson and Pearcey, "The dominant worldview today is naturalism, which has created a culture that is both post-Christian and post-modern. By post-Christian, we do not mean Americans no longer profess to be Christians or no longer attend church. As a matter of fact, most Americans do both. Rather, by *post-Christian* we mean that Americans, along with most other Western cultures, no longer rely on Judeo-Christian truths as the basis of their public philosophy or their consensus."[5] This is undoubtedly the result of the secularization of the American university, and presents concrete evidence of the power of curriculum design.

Studies have shown that the Gospel message from the early years of Christianity has been misunderstood, misrepresented, and taught through various heretical or unscriptural methods. Our academic institutions (both religious and secular) have either explicitly or implicitly influenced the current philosophy of religion in our culture. This philosophy is one that embraces a theology that denies the existence of Almighty God and has evolved into an age of pluralism, secularism, and occultism. What is being taught in the academic departments of our Colleges and Universities? How can Christian educators integrate spiritual life with their academic expertise and theological understanding? These are some of the probing questions that have been raised in the evangelical community.

How has Truth been Attacked in Academic Curricular?

Examination of curriculum materials in higher education prove that truth is under fire in American education. Truth, by definition, means that which reflects factual and/or spiritual reality (for a more complete definition see the Glossary). The world of academia has waged war against truth, and its fruit can be seen in literature, science, and psychology and in the broad array of courses in the humanities. The following are examples of how this is taking place in the aforementioned academic disciplines.

Literature Curriculum in Higher Education

An analysis of the college textbooks being used in required disciplines such as literature reveal some astounding facts about the propaganda of some English departments at major universities. The adoption of such materials is often done in the name of multicultural education and diversity; however, many of these texts reflect anti-Christian sentiments. The analysis of these materials is in no way an attack on freedom of expression or an indictment of the teaching at any particular academic institution but an observation of what is being taught in some university classrooms. The following is an examination of written texts that express modern and postmodern views.

Modernism and Post-Modernism[6]

Marked by a shift towards technological change and a rejection of Victorian ideals, the Modernist era coincided with the onset of World War II and marked a turning point in human thinking. According to Barton and Hudson, the "horrors of the First World War (1914-1918) served to deepen the loss of faith in the old orders of Western civilization."[7] These changes were expressed in many ways by artists and manifested themselves in expressions of fascination and alienation of traditional values. As a result of these changes, many writers began to experiment with different styles of writing. Would-be authors and poets abandoned the fuzzy, dreamy images of Romanticism and instead embraced a "direct treatment of the thing."[8] This move towards depicting reality in the most truthful way possible permeated all of modernist literature.

Thomas Hardy's "Ah, Are you Digging on My Grave?" is a prime example of a modernist style that has rejected the fuzzy, dreamy images of Romanticism. Hardy, who has been called a pessimist by many critics, is known for his treatment of life's bitter ironies within his pieces. *Ah, Are you Digging on My Grave?* is no exception. Told from the point of view of a deceased persona, the poem seeks to solve a mystery of sorts as the deceased tries to find out who is digging at her grave. Several times, the persona tries to guess the digger's identity and relationship to her, and several times, she comes up empty-handed as everyone is simply too busy to be bothered with her, "Then who is digging on my grave?/ My dearest kin? - Ah, no; they sit and think, what use!/What good will planting flowers produce?/No tendance of her mound can loose/ Her spirit from Death's gin."[9] Near the end of the poem the persona is relieved to find that the digger was in fact her faithful dog; however, even this is not an act of loyalty but merely means for the forgetful dog to bury his bone. In a tone that is both sarcastic and humorous, Hardy was commenting on the futility of man and on how meaningless life is. Further, Hardy was lamenting on the unfaithfulness of man as seen in the way that the deceased persona's loved ones easily forgot her.

Another mark of the modernist era was a change in women's roles in society as well as a change in attitudes towards women.

Yet, even as all of these changes were taking place, there were still several changes that needed to take place in regard to societal norms and standards. In response to the need for reform as well as a request to comment on the subject of women and fiction, Virginia Woolf wrote "A Room of One's Own." Within this piece, Woolf argues that a woman cannot effectively write fiction (or write as well as a man) unless she has money and a room of her own. According to Woolf, this is because, "if a woman wrote [in the early nineteenth century], she would have to write in the common sitting-room" where "she was always interrupted and never had a half hour that she could call her own."[10] Thus as a fellow woman and advocate, Woolf attempted to move women to action and to encourage them to seek financial independence and self-expression through fiction. This she said, would establish depictions of women in fiction that are created by other women rather than by men. Having experienced what it feels like to work hard to earn a living and what it feels like to have a fixed income, Woolf remarked, "I need not hate any man; he cannot hurt me. I need not flatter any man; he has nothing to give me (2000, p. 2173)."[11]

Following modernism, the literary world experienced another change in regards to literature called postmodernism. Postmodernism is a term describing a wide-ranging change in thinking beginning in the early twentieth century. Although a difficult term to define, 'postmodern' generally refers to the criticism of absolute truths or identities and "grand narratives." R. Wesley Hurd writes, "Perhaps the most general characteristics of postmodernism are fragmentation and pluralism. Our culture is rapidly reaching the point where we no longer think of ourselves in a *universe* but rather a *multi-verse*. In the postmodern worldview, transience, flux, and fragmentation describe our growing sense of how things really are."[12] Barton and Hudson, describe postmodernism as, "an age transformed by information technology, shaped by electronic images, and fascinated by popular culture."[13] From postmodernism other related topics such as relativism, decolonization, and selflessness emerge.

Oranges are Not the Only Fruit by Jeanette Wintersen (1985) is an example of a postmodern text. Written in an autobiographical style, the book draws on Wintersen's evangelical upbringings to tell the story of the protagonist, also called Jeannette and her journey through adolescence. Within this text, the headstrong protagonist is faced with a difficult decision, as she must decide whether or not she will pursue her "alternative, sexual" lifestyle or if she will follow the religious beliefs of her conservative upbringing. Faced with sharp criticism from her mother, pastor, and fellow parishioners, Jeannette decides that she can still love God and her lover Katy. Underlying the story of Jeannette is a more important issue of whether or not there is an absolute truth. As Jeannette herself has put it, she grew up in a home where, "there were no mixed feelings. There were friends and there were enemies."[14] To take the illustration a step further, one could argue that there were saints and there were sinners. While some of the doctrines and beliefs in the text appeared to be quite extreme, "Fruit salad, fruit pie, fruit for fools, fruited punch. Demon fruit, passion fruit, rotten fruit, fruit on Sunday. Oranges are the only fruit;"[15] Jeannette was convicted of the truth of most of what she was taught. The only conflict it seems had to do with the perfection of man and the issue of homosexuality. In the end, Jeannette chose to create her own truth so to speak. She states, "Everyone who tells a story tells it differently, just to remind us that everyone sees it differently. Some people say there are true things to be found, some people say all kinds of things can be proved. I don't believe them."[16] This falls in line with postmodern relativism which states that "the notion of truth is subject to time, place, and context."[17] Ironically, at the end of the story, Jeannette's mother appears to have relaxed her religious standards a bit even though she does not openly admit it.

The twentieth century has gone through several periods, which have drastically affected the literature of each era. The Modernist period has been concerned with a rejection of tradition values and a depiction of reality in the most truthful way possible; whereas the postmodern period has been concerned with a redefinition or the relativity of truth. Both eras saw changes in regards to technology and the information age. Post-colonialism, which was borne as a response to colonialism has also been concerned with truth as it relates to the way in which the colonial world is viewed. Each period has produced literature that has indelibly left its mark on generations to come.

Science Curriculum in Higher Education

Another subject worthy of discussion, as it relates to the American university's shift to secularism is the acceptance of evolution as a scientific fact. Authors Ché Ahn and Lou Engle said it well when they wrote:

When Charles Darwin wrote *The Origins of the Species*, he dropped a bomb upon the earth. He declared war on the truth, formulating a picture that all creation evolved from simple matter to complex matter – that humanity was not created in the image of God but that all creation evolved from a piece of protoplasm, so to speak. The so-called wise of this world believed the lie and foolishly removed God as Creator from public education. Darwin's theory promotes the belief that: "You're an accident! There's no Creative Designer of your life. You're only the result of natural processes.[18]

Christian scholars around the world understand the devastating effect of the Darwinist philosophy on the scientific enterprise but fail to underscore its prevalence in academia and how pervasive it is within the majority of science textbooks.

Scientific Inquiry at the University

The theory of evolution, as an explanation for the origin of the world and its inhabitants, has such credence today that it is broadly unacceptable to teach, as scientific theory, anything else. As a result, most people reject the scientific validity of any attempt to link life's origins with non-material causes.[19] In *Think Biblically: Recovering a Christian Worldview*, Chemistry professor, Dr. Taylor Jones wrote an article entitled "Why a Scriptural View of Science," in which he addressed the impact of science in terms of what it produces and its influence on how we think.[20]

When exploring the issue of scientific and philosophical inquiry, Dr. Jones wrote the following:

The goal of any philosophical inquiry should be the development or refinement of a general worldview that is correct; i.e., it must be consistent with an accurate picture of reality. This goal might sound ridiculously self-evident, but few people have even considered that they have a worldview, much less whether it is correct. Although there are many worldviews, not all of them can be correct. A worldview that is correct must be true, an expression of the way things really are. An incorrect worldview is of little value other than being amusing, interesting, or even fascinating. Although such incorrect views might provide a wealth of study for philosophers, they cannot provide much insight into how to live one's life. Since we have to live in a real universe with real people and real situations, a worldview that does not correctly interpret and reflect the way things are has little practical value. An enormously elaborate and complex map of roads and highways that are incorrectly depicted on a page will never help us navigate successfully from a journey's beginning to its final destination. So it is with aberrant worldviews. They only end up producing lost people.

If we go a step further and consider those aspects of the universe that intersect with the various disciplines of science, the same guidelines for assessing reliability must necessarily apply. The only difference here is that the scope of the investigation has been narrowed to things germane to science. One is still seeking a worldview of science that accurately describes and reliably reflects reality.[21]

Much of the scientific curriculums in our college and university classrooms have been tainted by the philosophical infiltration of Darwinist theory. College professors across the U.S. who have embraced the biblical concept of the six-day literal creation as cited in the book of Genesis have been the subject of ill treatment because of their convictions. The total rejection of the Genesis account is indeed a clear indication of the deceitfulness of human philosophy (Colossians 2:8). "The philosophical bankruptcy of philosophical thought has indeed left a void that was soon filled with ideas of another kind, coming from ill-digested science or pseudo-science."[22] This has poisoned theology and ethics in academia beyond any hope of immediate recovery, [23] save that science is reclaimed from Darwinism.

In his book *Science and the Bible*, Dr. Henry M. Morris president of the Institute of Creation Research, refuted Darwinism and the theory of evolution eloquently, when he wrote the following:

> More than one hundred years ago, Charles Darwin achieved lasting fame by publishing *The Origin of the Species*. Yet it is now recognized that, in that book, he never gave one specific example of the origin of any new species of plant or animal. He discussed numerous examples of "variation" within species and indulged in many speculations as to how different organisms might have evolved in the past, along with various notions as to possible relationships deduced from similarities, but he never gave any real proof of genuine *vertical* evolution. Yet, his speculative theory of unlimited variation and gradual accumulation of favorable variations by natural selection was soon accepted the world over as proof that all things had come into being by evolution.
> It is significant that, even at this late date, well over a century after Darwin and despite the lifelong efforts of thousands of scientists and untold millions of dollars spent on elaborate studies and experiments, evolutionists still have never experimentally observed the evolution of a single new species, nor do they have any certain knowledge of the mechanism by which evolution works. This is an amazing situation for a phenomenon that is widely promoted as one of the verities of modern science. There is certainly no parallel to this situation else in science.[24]

With the debate over evolution and the concept of creation regaining strength in the academic circle, there has been a concerted effort on the part of evolutionists to silence the voice of those in the scientific and religious community who believe in Creative Design or Intelligent Design. Christian scientists across this country and around the world have the responsibility to engage the culture and uphold the banner of truth, by communicating the scientific evidences as well as the theological truths that there is a Creator (God) to whom all men must give an account (I Peter 4:4-5). The philosophical vacuum left by evolutionists must be filled by the freedom found in the truth (John 8:32) of a living and loving God.

The Behavioral Sciences and Humanities in Higher Education

We should take care not to make the intellect our God; it has,
of course, powerful muscles, but no personality.
~ *Albert Einstein* ~

No fields in academia have succumbed to the humanism of the age more than the behavioral sciences, the social sciences, and the humanities, namely the liberal arts. The arms of psychology most often guide the liberal arts, (i.e. languages, literature, history, philosophy, mathematics, and science), which provide information of general cultural concern.

A basic definition of psychology is the science that deals with mental processes and behavior.[25] Psychology is a highly complex field of study that deals with both animal and human behavior. Nowhere is the fallacy of human reasoning more evident than in the field of psychology. Psychology as a field has embraced humanistic approaches to dealing with emotional and mental issues, since it is by nature a people-centered field. At a more abstract level, psychology is the study of the emotional and behavioral characteristics of an individual, a group, or an activity. Psychology is simultaneously socially motivated and inherently individualistic.

The Nature of Psychology

The purpose of this section is to provide a Christian perspective on the nature of psychology. This analysis will establish the fact that secular paradigms offer a limited view of psychological reality and that a Christian perspective brings an added and necessary dimension.

The contemporary nature of psychology can be likened to the art of building a high rise: a number of foundational truths or skeletal frameworks have been formative as the discipline has developed over the years. As a field of study, scientific psychology is little more than a hundred years old.[26] However, though at any one time there may be a dominant paradigm, there has not been paradigm succession. Rather elements of the older paradigms co-exist, if uncomfortably, with the newer ones. The impact of secular humanism in the field of psychology is the subject of our discussion.

Psychology and the behavioral sciences have devastating effects when they are not guided with the compassion of a caring and redemptive God. Dr. John D. Street addressed the conflict between theology and psychology when he wrote:

> The historical distrust and innate hostility between psychology and theology exist because each calls the legitimacy of the other's *Weltanschauung*. The imperialistic intrusion of the psychotherapeutic into Christianity has attempted to undermine and redefine the supremacy of the Word of God among Christians. Nowhere have its effects been more intrusive and dramatic than in the ministry of the Word in relation to pastoral soul-care.
>
> For over a century graduate schools and seminaries have trained an army of pastoral students in a variety of psychologies under the tenets of some renowned psychologist or psychotherapist, or worse, taught an academic smorgasbord of psychological methods and theories from which the pastor could draw as he saw fit. Some of the most influential, early psychologies in theological graduate schools included the psychoanalysis of Sigmund Freud, the analytical psychology of Carl Jung, the nondirective psychotherapeutic counseling of Carl Rogers, the physiological psychology of the liberal theologian-turned-psychologist G. T. Ladd, and the existential psychology of Soren Kierkegaard. Pastors, trained under these psychologies, influenced an entire generation of parishioners to think and act according to the therapeutic instead of according to the Gospel. Even the authorial intent

of Scripture was replaced by psychological hermeneutic that loaded biblical terminology with psychotherapeutic meaning. Where the Bible was not replaced by a psychology, it was redefined by it.[27]

An investigation of the field of psychology informs us that the existence of God has been circumstantially denied, and that man is placed at the center of the universe. The self-aggrandizement of man is evidence of the fallacies of human reasoning and the depravity of man. Dr. R.C. Sproul was right when he wrote in, *The Psychology of Atheism*:

> Atheists often dismiss the Christian's belief in God as a direct result of psychological need. "If God does not exist," they ask, "why are people so religious?" We desire to pose the same question back to them: If there is a God, why are there atheists? And our answer is similar to theirs, except that the Scriptures offer a far more persuasive case than, for example, the embarrassing psychoanalysis of Sigmund Freud. In *Civilization and Its Discontents*, Freud wrote that religious needs derive from "the infant's helplessness and the longing for the father" and that this vulnerability is permanently sustained by "fear of the superior power of Fate." Quite to the contrary, we believe that those like Freud who reject God do so in order to escape the helplessness that one feels in the face of the holy and "superior power" of the God who really exists.[28]

Nowadays, the culture has used the psychological nuances of humanism to be free from any form of accountability. In the pursuit of human happiness and guilt free living, the self-esteem, self-help, self-worth, psychotherapist gurus of the world have managed to do away with human decency and human responsibility. Dr. John F. MacArthur, Jr. addressed this psychosocial dilemma when he said:

> That kind of thinking has all but driven words like *sin, repentance, contrition, atonement, restitution*, and *redemption* out

of the public discourse. If no one is supposed to feel guilty, how could anyone be a sinner? Modern culture has the answer: people are *victims*. Victims are not responsible for what they do; they are casualties of what happens to them. So every human failing must be described in terms of how the perpetrator has been victimized. We are all supposed to be "sensitive" and "compassionate" enough to see that the very behaviors we used to label "sin" are actually evidence of victimization.[29]

The result of such practice and acceptance of false human tolerance that has swept through the academic community is even now prevalent in the religious community and the Church and is the byproduct of the humanistic teaching, taking place across the humanities. The feel good, do as you want philosophy that has inundated the minds of the educated as well as the illiterate in our culture, has resulted in a God-less society with a total disregard for morality, ethics, and that which is absolute. Christians across Christendom, particularly Christian Educators, must understand that it is our God-given mandate to take charge in the battle for the human mind by "casting down arguments and every high thing that exalts itself against the knowledge of God, [by] bringing every thought into captivity to the obedience of Christ" (II Corinthians 10:4-5).

NOTES

[1] Pamela J. Farris, *Teaching, Bearing the Torch*. (Boston, MA: McGraw-Hill College, 1999), 34.

[2] Allan C. Ornstein and Daniel U. Levine, *Foundations of Education*. (Boston, MA: Houghton Mifflin Company, 2000), 453.

[3] John S. Park and Gayle D. Beebe (Editors), *Religion and Its Relevance in Post-Modernism: Essays in honor of Jack C. Verheyden.* (Lewiston, NY: The Edwin Mellen Press, 2001), 77.

[4] Darwin K. Glassford, *Toward a Theological Foundation for Christian Higher Education*, 1. Retrieved on June 6, 2003 from http://capo.org/premise/96/mj/p960507.html.

[5] Charles Colson and Nancy Pearcy, *How now shall we live?* (Wheaton, IL: Tyndale House Publishers, 2001), 22.

[6] Part of this text was adopted from a paper written by my wife, Marsha Valmyr on "*Modernism, Postmodernism and Post-colonialism*" for a graduate English course, entitled Voices in Twentieth Century British literature, dated from February, 2006.

[7] E.J. Barton and G.A. Hudson, *A Contemporary Guide to Literary Terms*. (New York: Houghton Mifflin Company, 1997), 122.

[8] M.H. Abrams, et al. (Eds.) *The Norton Anthology of English literature*, Volume 2 (7th ed.). (New York: W.W. Norton & Company, 2000), 1902.

[9] Ibid, 1946.

[10] Ibid, 2188.

[11] Ibid, 2173.

[12] R. Wesley Hurd, *Postmoderninsm* Article quoted from *McKenzie Study Center*; an institute of Gutenberg College. Retrieved on April 23, 2007 from http://www.mckenziestudycenter.org/philosophy/articles/postmod.html

[13] E.J. Barton and G.A. Hudson, *A Contemporary Guide to Literary Terms*. (New York: Houghton Mifflin Company, 1997), 166.

[14] Jeanette Wintersen, *Oranges are not the only fruit*. (New York: The Atlantic Monthly Press, 1985), 3.

[15] Ibid, 29.

[16] Ibid, 93.

[17] E.J. Barton and G.A. Hudson, *A Contemporary Guide to Literary Terms*. (New York: Houghton Mifflin Company, 1997),166.

[18] Ché Ahn and Lou Engle, *The Call Revolution: A Radical Invitation to Turn the Heart of a Nation back to God*. (Colorado Springs, CO: Wagner Publications, 2001), 32.

[19] David F. Dawes. *Design or Chance*. Article quoted from *Faith Today*, (January/February 2004); an online magazine published by the Evangelical Fellowship of Canada. Retrieved July 28, 2006 from http://www.faithtoday.ca/article_viewer.asp? *Article_ID=109*.

[20] John MacArthur (General editor) and Richard Mayhue. *Think Biblically: Recovering a Christian Worldview*. (Wheaton, IL: Crossway Books, 2003), 221.

[21] l Ibid, 221.

[22] Taken from an article entitled *Science, Postmodernism, and Philosophy* by Warren Murray. Alice Ramos and Marie I. George

(editors). *Faith, Scholarship, and Culture in the 21ˢᵗ Century.* (Washington, D.C.: American Maritain Association, 2002), 129.

[23] Ibid, 129.

[24] Henry M. Morris. *Science and the Bible (Revised and Updated).* (Chicago, IL.: Moody Press, 186), 44-45.

[25] John MacArthur (General editor) and Richard Mayhue. *Think Biblically: Recovering a Christian Worldview.* (Wheaton, IL: Crossway Books, 2003), 209.

[26] Gary R. Collins. *Christian Counseling: A Comprehensive Guide.* (Nashville, TN: W. Publishing Group, 1988), 22.

[27] Taken from an article entitled *Why Biblical Counseling and Not Psychology* by John D. Street. John MacArthur (General editor) and Richard Mayhue. *Think Biblically: Recovering a Christian Worldview.* (Wheaton, IL: Crossway Books, 2003), 204.

[28] R.C. Sproul, *Defending Your Faith: An Introduction to Apologetics.* (Wheaton, IL: Crossway Publishing, 2003), 159.

[29] John MacArthur, *The Vanishing Conscience.* (Dallas, TX: Word Publishing, 1994), 21.

PART FOUR

ISSUES

&

SOLUTIONS

CHAPTER 7

THEOLOGICAL ANALYSIS OF ISSUES RELATED TO WORLDVIEW FORMATION

—ɯ—

Spiritual Issues (Origin of man)

The origin of man is perhaps the greatest question that has been raised across higher education as much literature in postsecondary education has touched on this subject. Specifically our views of man have permeated into the development of various worldviews that deny the existence of a loving God who is the Creator and Maker of all things and to whom we are all accountable.

The origin of man is one of the critical (spiritual and scientific) issues in educational worldview theories. The worldviews of this generation are intrinsically related to the moral mores of this society and are often the expression of our culture. In an analysis of the current state of the American culture, Charles Colson and Nancy Pearcey made the following comments:

> Americans have reached "the modernist impasse": They were told they had a right to be free from the restrictions of morality and religion, yet as unrestricted choices have led to social breakdown, they have begun to long for the protection that morality once provided. After all, we didn't

have epidemics of crime, broken families, abortion, or sexually transmitted diseases when Americans largely accepted biblical morality. Many are beginning to understand that morality is not merely an arbitrary constraint on individual choice but a protection against social disintegration.

That's why, after decades of public rhetoric about individual rights, we now hear cultural leaders struggling to find some common secular language to revive a sense of civic duty and virtue.[1]

The spiritual, social, and scientific issues presented by the assumption that God did not create man have various moral consequences. As discussed in previous chapters, the educational community has been engaged in various hidden agendas to ignore Blaise Pascal's assumption that, "There is a God shaped vacuum in the heart of every man." By contrast, the idea of creative design is evident in various scientific inquiries.

Doctrinal Issues (Faith and Reason)

The quarrel between theology and science has been at the center of academic debates for centuries. Further, doctrinal issues are a major concern for most academic institutions of higher learning. For instance, the issue of creation is one of many doctrinal issues in both Christian and secular academic institutions. The most central of all these issues is the debate between faith and reason, religion and academia, theism (God as Creator) and Darwinism or, to put it in laymen's terms, creation and evolution.

While this is true of Christian institutions, secular institutions seem to have a hidden agenda of their own when it comes to the Christian worldview of life. In an article entitled *Our Listless Universities*, author Allan Bloom wrote:

Students in our best universities do not believe in anything, and those universities are doing nothing about it, nor can they. An easygoing American Nihilism has descended upon us, a nihilism without terror of the Abyss. The great questions of –God, freedom, and immortality, according to Kant— hardly touch the young. And the universities, which should encourage for the clarification of such questions, are the very source of the doctrine which makes that quest appear futile. The heads of the young are stuffed with a jargon derived from the despair of European thinkers, gaily repackaged for American consumption and presented as the foundation for a pluralistic society. That jargon becomes a substitute for real experiences and instinct; one suspects that modern thought has produced an artificial soul to replace the old one supplied by nature, which was full of dangerous longings, loves, hates, and awes. The new soul's language consists of terms like *value*, *ideology*, *self*, *commitment*, *identity*—every word derived from recent German philosophy, and each carrying a heavy baggage of dubious theoretical interpretation of which its users are blissfully unaware. They take such language to be as unproblematic and immediate as night and day. It now constitutes our peculiar common sense.[2]

Allan Bloom's point in the aforementioned article is that students today don't really believe in anything and that when they do, they don't know why they believe it. Unfortunately, modern university, which should be the solution, is often part of the problem. Most colleges no longer provide a true liberal arts education or most faculty no longer encourage their students to approach the material with an open mind or to avoid the fashionable idea of the moment if neces- sary and to judge everything on its own merits or demerits, based on real experience and a reading of the great ideas of history. George M. Marsden, author of *The Soul of the American University*, echoed the same sentiments expressed by Bloom by outlining the source of liberalism in American higher education. In a piece entitled *"The Elusive Ideas of Academic Freedom"*, Marsden wrote:

The direct inspiration for the modern American concep- tion of academic freedom came, however, from Germany, or at least from the romanticized impressions of Germany that many thousands of American academics who studied there brought back with them. Particularly important for the American organizers of the academic profession after 1890 was the German *Lehrfreiheit*, referring to freedom for university professors. In Germany this freedom included, first, the rights for university professors to teach whatever they chose with a minimum of administrative regulations and, second, the freedom to conduct one's research and to report one's findings in lectures and publications without external restraint. At the heart of *Lehrfreiheit*, as Americans typically understood it, was the modern ideal that truth is progressive and that for science to advance it must be freed from tradition and preconception.... Once the wider applications of modern *Lehrfreiheit* were accepted, however, they were proclaimed by their protestant advocates as essential to any institution calling itself a "university."[3]

The view of academic freedom as a sacred concept has had its benefits as well its devastating effects on the American university. Academic freedom has been the focal point of the debate between faith and reason, religion and the academics, Christian theism and naturalism. For the Christian educator, academic freedom must also include the freedom to present a Christian worldview of life, one that views God as sovereign over all knowledge and transcendent over all things.

NOTES

[1] Charles Colson and Nancy Pearcey. *How Now Shall We Live?* (Wheaton, IL: Tyndale House Publishers, 1999), 310-311.

[2] Taken from the article first printed in the National Review, December 10, 1982 Educational Excellence Network Vol. II, No. 4. March, 1983. Reprinted in Network News & Views Vol. XV, No. 12 December 1996.

[3] George M. Marsden, *The Soul of the American University: From Protestant Establishment to Established Nonbelief.* (Oxford, UK: Oxford University Press, 1994), 297.

CHAPTER 8

Principal Factors

—ϻ—

Educators' Scholarship Level and Background

The development of worldviews in higher education is a very important topic for the twenty-first century Christian. In the words of Ronald Nash, "A worldview is a conceptual scheme by which we consciously place or fit everything we believe and by which we interpret and judge reality."[1] The factors that influence worldview development in education are the educators' scholarship level and background.

The biographical, educational backgrounds and moral convictions of higher education faculties have always played a major role in their teaching careers. Though lack of proper support and short-sightedness on the part of the education policy makers is a major factor that has contributed to the decline of authentic liberal arts education in America, the educational backgrounds of educators themselves are often contributing in no small measure to this decline by their lack of exposure to western tradition and literature. Given the current state of our culture, two important changes have to be brought about in order to ensure that the next generation of leaders is equipped to face the cultural challenges to come in the near future. These changes include making graduates more equipped to make wise judgments in the world of ideas and to impact the cultural and moral vision of society by promoting values of ethics and virtue.

Globally, the socio-political and/or educational agenda is now increasingly being driven by the invasion of non-Christian ideas in all academic disciplines. In the current scheme of things, academic credentials are becoming far more important than any other factor and the number of students enrolled is the measuring stick for success in higher education. Consequently, education is becoming more and more secular while the educational enterprise is becoming increasingly narrow-minded on issues of morality and virtue. In short, it is an enterprise where anything other than Christianity is tolerated.

It is now clear that universities are not just independent institutions of learning. As important organs of civil society, they form part of the matrix of key societal ideas and policy, which contribute to shaping cultural, economic, and scientific development. It is with this notion in mind that higher education students must exercise prudence and discernment about what they are being taught. In a broader sense, students must be very selective about what they allow to become part of their worldview.

Category of School (Religious Stands & Philosophical views)

In our previous discussion on American higher education in the colonial era, we touched on the beginnings of academic institutions in America (see Chapter 2). Since its inception, higher education in America has always been connected to the social movements of the culture. Institutions of higher learning can be categorized as public or private, religiously affiliated or non-religiously affiliated, non-evangelical denominational or evangelical Christian institutions. While higher education institutions in the United States are diverse in terms of highest degree granted (associate's, bachelor's, master's, doctorate), institutional control (public or private), size, mission, and learning environment; there are generally two characteristics that impact the student the most, namely the religious and philosophical stand of the academic institution. The educational philosophy of any institution of higher learning is of grave importance to the learner. Schools often adopt institutional values that express their religious and philosophical stands on life and society. Harry Lee Poe said it well when he wrote the following:

Alongside religion, philosophical ideas permeate the academy, although we are not always aware of their presence or impact. Religion and philosophy interact with and influence each other, although often unintentional and unconsciously. Whether we are aware of it or not, philosophy runs through every discipline of the academy. Indeed, prevailing philosophies may so dominate disciplines that identify the values of the philosophical position with the discipline. Ironically, the philosophy may be hidden under so many layers of "what everybody knows" that we do not even recognize its presence.[2]

Recognizing that all learners can fall prey to pre-conceived or pre-conditioned concepts that are established in the instructional philosophy of academic institutions, it is important to examine some of the belief systems that greatly influence the activities of learners. Therefore, Christian educators teaching in secular and religiously affiliated institutions of higher learning must ensure to enhance and contribute to conversations about religion in higher education across all types of post secondary institutions.

NOTES

[1] Ronald H. Nash, *Worldviews in Conflicts: Choosing Christianity in a World of Ideas.* (Grand Rapids, MI: Zondervan Publishing House, 1992), 16.

[2] Harry Lee Poe, *Christianity in the Academy: Teaching at the Intersection of Faith and Learning.* (Grand Rapids, MI: Baker Academics, 2004), 21.

CHAPTER 9

Teaching Pedagogy

—∿∿—

Teaching and Learning

Teaching and learning is a life-long process that is driven by a sense of curiosity and the desire to acquire the knowledge necessary to live successfully. This process is a progressive inter-action between educators and their constituents. The progressivism philosophy is implemented by developing curricula that aim at changing the way of life.

The scope of any academic curricula must transmit practical knowledge and problem-solving skills by feeding on the learners' needs, interests, and unlimited potential to be developed through education. For instance, progressivism (see Chapter 2) as an educa-tional theory is a non-authoritarian theory of education that focuses on the individual as well as the collective success of our educa-tional enterprises. As Christian educators, our focus should be on students' needs (spiritual, intellectual, and physical), not on self or merely on content area. Inadvertently, college students usually focus on their personal aspirations in life (individualism, careers, and personal freedom) and the deeper meaning of how things are going to affect them (personal philosophy of life). Therefore, the educational journey for the Christian educator must be a partner-ship that embraces teaching and learning creatively by developing life skills aimed at using knowledge wisely and practically in every aspect of life (wisdom). The main focus of the progressive curriculum is that learning can be promoted in the educational context and lead to greater motivation and skill development. Teaching has the potential to transform lives, not just by providing students with an opportunity to learn the tools of academic success but by imparting wisdom for daily living. Moreover, the greater potential of teaching lies in the ability to change the future of countless lives and to form men and women of integrity. This approach is not limited to the classroom setting but includes extra-curricular activities such as mentoring and coaching.

Teaching Students How to Learn

The dynamics of student interaction with curriculum and instruction is a national obsession in education. Student interactions have been directly linked to teaching and learning. The teaching practices of educators have received the attention of education theorists and are worth thinking about in relation to higher education. Looking at knowledge and the use of knowledge as a way of conceptualizing the instructional process or curriculum phenomena can be very helpful in shedding light on the ways educators teach or impart knowledge, specifically in the area of worldviews. After all, messages come to students over time during the many years of schooling that stipulate the control of educators, particularly in higher education. The direction controls of the educational process are described in the five roles of educators. These roles are learning and teaching, personal supports, collegial relationships, management efficiency, and school leadership and advocacy.

Methods of Teaching

The oldest and most widely used method of teaching in universities worldwide is the lecture. Over time, ideas about effective practices of lecturing have emerged. According to McKeachie and Svinicki, the most "effective lecturers combine talents of scholar, writer, producer, comedian, entertainer, and teacher in ways that contribute to learning."[1] Despite these findings however, very few lecturers apply these principles to their classroom teaching as McKeachie and Svinicki state that even the best lecturers are not always in top form.

After the lecture, the next most widely used teaching method is probably the seminar. The active nature of the seminar makes it the main source for students to acquire some of the personal transferable skills, e.g. in presentation and group work. In addition, the advent of technology in the classroom has brought other methods of teaching into the educational enterprise. Methods such as computer-assisted instruction, online learning and computer enhanced instruction have emerged as part of the latest development in teaching and learning. The face of education, particularly that of higher education, has been changing so rapidly that educators must keep up with the latest innovations in computer technology. The lecture method however, in spite of the advent of numerous developments in technology, has stood the test of time.

Research on the Effectiveness of Lectures[2]

A large number of studies have compared the effectiveness of lectures with other teaching methods. The results are discouraging for those who lecture. Discussion methods are superior to lectures in student retention of information after the end of a course; in transfer of knowledge to new situations; in development of problem solving, thinking, or attitude change; and in motivation for further learning (McKeachie et al., 1990).

Similarly, print offers advantages over lecture. Students can read faster than lecturers can lecture, and they can go back when they don't understand, skip material that is irrelevant, and review immediately or later. Lectures go at the lecturer's pace, and students who fall behind are out of luck. Despites these findings however, lectures can still be useful however.

Nature Vs. Nurture

The nature verses nurture debate has been around for centuries. This historical debate was focused on the issue of whether human intelligence is inherited or developed. While the issue of how differences in intelligence come about in individuals and groups is a topic of controversy in the field of psychology, it has played a great role in the arena of teaching and learning.

Historically, educational theorists have argued on both sides of the aisle when it comes to the abilities of the human mind. In looking at the causes of individual differences in intelligence[3], a major issue is the relative contribution of genetics (nature) and the environment (nurture). Without entering the current debate, let us examine the relationship of nature and nurture within the contexts of worldview development. While one may argue for the concept of nature (genetic inheritance) or one may argue for the idea of nurture (environmental influence); the general consensus in worldview development is that worldviews are mostly developed through the influence of various external forces or nurture.

Ken Smitherman, President of the Association of Christian Schools International supports the idea that worldviews are taught and are thus, a result of external influence.[4]

He writes:

> Students give evidence of a biblical worldview not only as they develop a deeper understanding of biblical concepts but also as they then give expression to those concepts. For example, students would understand the worth of every human being as created in the image of God, possess apologetic skill to defend their faith in God, and have the ability to articulate and defend their own biblical worldview while having at least a basic understanding of opposing worldviews.

> The teaching, training, and nurturing of students toward their development of a continuously maturing worldview should also foster in them a commitment to lifelong learning—a desire to continue to explore, learn about, and experience God's creation and provision for His people. You see, the formal Christian school experience is not intended to be a culmination of learning but rather a motivation to grow and learn throughout an entire lifetime.

In light of our current discussion, it is inherently important to consider the God-given responsibility and power of the teaching profession in shaping the minds of an entire generation. In the words of Plato, "Education is not what the profession of certain men assert it to be. They presumably assert they put into the soul knowledge that isn't in it, as though they were putting sight into blind eyes."[5] The influence of teaching is not one that is based on just the transfer of information (stamping education), but one that aims at developing critical thinkers; thus, an education by which we train philosophers and men or women of virtue.

Teaching with Grace

The notion of grace within teaching practices is a concept that is mentioned throughout scripture. Consequently, one of the greatest topics in higher education as of late has been the concept of spirituality. The idea of teaching to produce a coherent Christian worldview of God, man and the world is a process that demands much thinking and practicality. Bruce A. Little writes the following about the need for Christians engaged in higher education to articulate a Christian worldview. He argues that Christians must develop a unified view of reality across the curriculum. He writes:

> Thinking integratively and coherently requires a conscious and strenuous effort even on the part of the instructor. Students need to be challenged with the importance of worldview thinking while denying them the luxury of simply maintaining their uncritical, fragmented thinking. Instead the student must be engaged by thought-provoking exercises where interpretative consistency is expected and logical extensions of beliefs unpacked. Courses should be Christian worldview oriented, encouraging students to view each piece of information in light of the whole. Information should not only be memorized but also intellectually related to the known to determine how or if it fits with a Christian worldview.[6]

While the aforementioned comments can be easily applied within the context of Christian education, it will require much wisdom to see this applied within the broader context of non-Christian education or in the secular classroom. Keeping in mind the idea of learning as a search for truth, those (Christians) who teach at the college level must explore the possibilities of teaching with grace by integrating faith in their teaching practices. Thus, Christian instructors have the duty to go beyond the acquisition of knowledge and must enter the realm of meaning and purpose. Whether this is to occur within the confines of the discipline or by engaging in interdisciplinary approaches of teaching and learning, is entirely up to the instructor.

NOTES

[1] Wilbert J. McKeachie and Marilla Svinicki, *McKeachie's Teaching Tips: Strategies, Research, and Theory for College and University Teachers.* (Boston, MA: Houghton Mifflin Company, 2006), 57.

[2] Ibid, 58.

[3] Intelligence theorists fall into two categories. In one group are those who argue for a "general intelligence," a single, general aptitude or ability. In the other are those who believe that intelligence is composed of many separate and distinct aptitude or abilities. Taken from Morris, Charles G. and Albert A. Maisto. *Psychology an Introduction (Eleventh Edition).* (Upper Saddle River, NJ: Prentice Hall, 2002), 346.

[4] Taken from Ken Smitherman, *Shaping a Worldview.* Christian School Comment Vol.38, Num. 2 (Colorado Springs, CO: Association Christian Schools International).

[5] Plato. *The Republic of Plato (Second Edition):Translated with Notes, and an Interpretive Essay and a New Introduction by Allan David Bloom.* (New York, NY: Basic Books, 1991), (518b-c) 197.

[6] Bruce A. Little, *Christian Education, Worldviews, and Postmodernity's Challenge.* (Lynchburg, VA: Journal of the Evangelical Theological Society, 1997, accessed March 15, 2006); available from http://www.etsjets.org/jets/journal/40/40-3/40-3-pp433-444_JETS.pdf

PART FIVE

RECOMMENDATIONS

CHAPTER 10

CONCLUSIONS

—⚊ᄿᄿᄿ⚊—

The premise of the entire book was based on the hypothesis that Christians have failed to preserve the Christian world-view in college campuses and have not effectively integrated the Christian faith into academic institutions. Many scholars indicate that Christians engaged in higher education have relinquished their roles in propagating the Christian worldview to a lost and perverse generation. The results of this dereliction have been catastrophic for at least three reasons. The first is that believers have only a piece-meal understanding of the Christian faith. The second is that such a piecemeal perspective shortchanges the Christian life and experi-ence. The third is that the Church has lost much of her effectiveness in terms of both personal witness and cultural impact.

While American Christians who attend college only spend an average of four to five hours per week in Church; they spend more than twelve to eighteen hours or more per week in the classroom and another twenty to forty hours working a part-time or full-time job. Without a solid biblical worldview, is it any wonder that believers are so anemic and indistinct and that the Church has such little influ-ence in shaping North American culture? The average, college-age student does not attend church regularly and has very little interest in developing a Christian worldview. The Church cannot wait for them to come to us; we must go to them either as professors in their college classrooms or as missionaries (campus chaplains/ ministers) on the college campus.

Although pressure points abound in academia, sustainable service is possible within the academic landscape by those who possess a Christian worldview. The believer can contribute towards the fulfillment of the Great Commission (Matthew 28:18-20) and the cultural mandate (Genesis 1:28). The potential to influence future generations is inherently present in the teaching-learning experience, while educating students to produce a God honoring *weltanschauung*, a worldview.

We have explored the relationship between worldviews in higher education and Christianity, and the integration of faith in teaching practices at the post-secondary level. Worldviews have been interpreted using two complementary analogies: an ontological analogy, i.e., belief about the nature of reality, and an epistemological one, i.e., method of knowledge and action. It is man's concept of truth that links these two analogies together in any culture. A number of key concepts developed in this book were based on literature on the history and philosophy of American higher education and helped to give clarity to change in the Western worldviews. Particular emphasis has been given to the change from a Judeo-Christian worldview to a pluralistic worldview.

Areas of conformity and conflict in beliefs have been identified pointing toward the thesis that the secularism of America is a direct result of the Christian community's abjuration of her God-given responsibility to impact the world for Christ (I Peter 4:15). This indictment is made with the acknowledgement that many Christian leaders have made exceptional contributions within Christendom in past centuries. Their efforts have led to various strategies aimed at effectively presenting a Christian response to the spiritual climate within American culture.

Implications of the Text

Christians (including parents, pastors, and teachers) engaged in the teaching profession cannot assume that the development of a Christian worldview is to occur in a vacuum, namely apart from the impartation of life-freeing principles of truth. Individuals (students) who may be behaving in a culturally-appropriate manner within their own cultural norms and values may be viewed as spiritually aberrant if viewed from the Christian perspective. If educators (Christian educators) interpret a student's thoughts, feelings, and personal convictions only through the lens of their own religious framework, those educators will not be responsive to the student's needs and, in fact, may not contribute to their spiritual formation.

It follows that the strategic approaches designed to address the manifestations of secular worldviews must be biblically and spiritually (Christ-centered) rooted and consistent. As stated by Dr. Ronald Nash (2004), "...No real progress towards improving American education can occur until all of us realize that an education that ignores moral and religious beliefs cannot qualify as quality education." This emphasizes the importance of consistency on biblically based philosophy of teaching (e.g., Lewis, 1980 and Proverbs 22:6) and the development of a philosophy of education that embraces the Christian worldview (Nash, 1988 and Sproul, 1986).

Related to these implications is the importance of educators to possess a general knowledge of the spiritual climate in the classroom, the students' spiritual background and related cultural heritage, including cultural traditions, social customs, philosophical understanding of life, languages, and value sets. There is a strong relationship between an individual's philosophy of life, and the teaching received in higher education.

The importance of using sound pedagogy in all disciplines in order to present a theistic approach to teaching through the integration of various practices such as prayer, Scripture, faith, forgiveness, and redemption is evident. The result of basing teaching practices on a theistic, Christ-centered and Spirit-led model could lead to significant transformation within the cultural landscape of our institutions of higher learning. This transformation must commence with the Christian educator and end with the students who come into their sphere of influence.

Last, this book provides support for the concept of merging worldview development within higher education through teaching and learning. Despite the various challenges that Christian educators face in secular and Christian institutions, the Great Commission, the biblical and cultural mandate demand a commitment to the renewal of the mind through education, irrespective of the discipline that the Christian educator teaches.

Recommendations

This book has been an attempt to ask and to find answers to the following questions: What is being taught in the academic departments of our colleges and universities? How can Christian educators integrate spiritual life within their academic expertise and theological understanding?

There are many things that could be done on a personal level to integrate the Christian worldview in academic institutions and the culture at large. The scripture enjoins Christians regardless of their profession to "sanctify the Lord God in your hearts, and [to] always be ready to give a defense to everyone who asks you a reason for the hope that is in you, with meekness and fear" (I Peter 3:15). The following are practical suggestions for Christians who want to take action.

Open Your Heart

Ask God to help you get a handle on any part of the fundamental teachings of Christianity that you have not fully embraced. Prayerfully repent and ask God to remove this unbelief out of your heart.

A sound biblical presentation of the Christian worldview begins in the heart, so that is where you must start. Ask God to open your heart to the issues of spiritual and worldview formation and accept the call to be an ambassador of Christ from now on, even if you don't understand the future ramifications of such a radical disposition.

Be a Foundation Builder

Think of three or four subjects in your area of discipline or line work where you can place yourself to begin to build a solid foundation for the development of a biblically sound worldview. For example, Christian educators can think about the potential that he or she has to impact a future generation of world leaders.

Befriend others in your spheres of influence who are different from you as the Lord provides the opportunities. Always be mindful that the Holy Spirit desires to use you right where you are, whether it is in the classroom, in the campus bookstore or on an athletic event.

Christian educators can extend invitations for dialogue with others in the profession who have different views on life and on religion. Remember that healthy dialogues can spark the curiosity of many who hold secular and non-theistic worldviews.

Be a Truth Dispenser

As a Christian educator, make it a matter of priority to always promote truth. Seek God for wisdom on how to apply the truth of God's word within your area of expertise. We are commanded by God to "let the Word of Christ dwell richly in you [us] richly in all wisdom..."so that we might be able to"... do all in the name of the Lord Jesus...." Colossians 3:16-17). Thus, the commitment to hide God's Word in the heart is not only the source of wisdom, but of power and of a sound mind.

Educate Yourself

Author Chip Ingram often encourages Christians to read great books.[1] Many worldview experts believe that reading books on various topics related to philosophy (Classical & Western), theology, religion, and various worldviews is critical for the process of learning and listening. Thus, they encourage a broad range of studies within the guise of reclaiming lost ground by returning to liberal arts and classical education. By reading this study, you have already moved in the right direction. A book list is provided in the bibliography to help you continue the journey.

Teach and Train

If you are a parent, a pastor, a youth leader or an educator, begin to think through your core values and mission in life to evaluate its consistency with the Christian worldview. Begin to teach those who are following you about your biblical perspective on philosophy and worldviews.

This book has many Bible references, literature, and research findings that will give you more than enough material to build on. Indeed, you are gifted beyond what is in this study to teach as God grants you special favor. Put the ideas found in the subjects of cultural reformation, secularism, cultural mandate, the Great Commission and the Christian worldview on your purpose and mission so that you can begin to open the eyes and ears of those whom you can influence.

NOTES

[1] Chip Ingram, *Good to Great in God's Eyes*. (Grand Rapids, MI: BakerBooks, 2007), 35-52.

APPENDICES

Appendix A

Sample Participant Background Survey

1. Sex: Male   Female

2. Age: (Mark one)
   16 or younger   21-24
   17   25-29
   18   30-39
   19   40-54
   20   55 or older

3. Have you placed your trust in Jesus Christ to save you from your sins and to give you eternal life?   Yes   No

4. If yes, how long have you been a Christian? (Mark one)
   1-5 years   21-30 years   over 60 years
   6-10 years   31-40 years
   11-15 years   41-50 years
   16-20 years   51-60 years

5. What is your current religious preference?
   Assemblies of God
   Baptist
   Buddhist
   Church of Christ
   Church of God
   Eastern Orthodox
   Episcopalian
   Full Gospel Charismatic
   Hindu
   Islamic
   Jewish
   Lutheran
   Methodist

Mormon
Non-Denominational
Pentecostal
Presbyterian
Quaker
Roman Catholic
Seventh Day Adventist
Unitarian/Universalist
United Church of Christ/Congregational
Other Religion
None

6. Have either of your parents placed their trust in Jesus Christ to save them from their sins and to give them eternal life?
   Yes   No

7. Please select the answer(s) that best reflects your educational background:
   (a)   I have only attended public school (elementary, jr. high, high)
   (b)   I attended both public and Christian schools (elementary, jr. high, high)
   (c)   I have only attended Christian schools (elementary, jr. high, high)
   (d)   I attended public school but I attended a Christian university
   (e)   I attended Christian school but attended a secular university
   (f)   I have attended a ministry training school/seminary

8. Are you currently enrolled in a college, professional school, or seminary? (Circle one)
   Yes   No

9. If yes, are you enrolled as a: (Circle one)
   Full-time student   Part-time student

10. What is the highest degree attained?
    I do not currently hold a degree

Vocational Certificate

Associate

Bachelor's degree

Master's degree

Ed. Specialist degree

PhD, D.Min., or Ed.D...

M.D., D.O., D.D.S., or D.V.M

J.D.

B.D. or M.DIV.

Other

11. What is the highest degree attained by your parents?

Father	Mother
My father does not currently hold a degree	My mother does not currently hold a degree
Vocational Certificate	Vocational Certificate
Associate	Associate
Bachelor's degree	Bachelor's degree
Master's degree	Master's degree
Ed. Specialist degree	Ed. Specialist degree
PhD, D.Min., or Ed.D	PhD, D.Min., or Ed.D
M.D., D.O., D.D.S., or D.V.M	M.D., D.O., D.D.S., or D.V.M
J.D.	J.D.
B.D. or MDIV.	B.D. or MDIV.
Other	Other

12. How would you describe your political views? (Mark one)

Liberal

Conservative

Neither liberal nor conservative

For each of the following statements, select the number on the continuum that best reflects your views:

5- Strongly agree   **4**- Agree Somewhat   **3**-Agree
2- Disagree Somewhat   **1**- Disagree

13. Any couple involved in a loving, monogamous relationship should have the right to marry regardless of sexual preference or orientation.

    5   4   3   2   1

14. Churches and other religious organizations spend too much time focusing on sin and repentance.

    5   4   3   2   1

15. The Biblical account of creation is true.

    5   4   3   2   1

16. God is distant and impersonal and thus is not interested in the daily affairs of man.

    5   4   3   2   1

17. Abortion should be available on-demand.

    5   4   3   2   1

18. My faith is the driving force behind all of my decisions.

    5   4   3   2   1

19. Creative Design should be taught in science curriculums at college and universities.

    5   4   3   2   1

20. Diversity and tolerance should be encouraged in Christian colleges and universities by allowing instructors of various religious preferences to serve as faculty.

          5   **4**   **3**   **2**   **1**

21. It doesn't matter what one believes as long as he or she is sincere in that belief.

          5   **4**   **3**   **2**   **1**

Appendix B

SAMPLE WORLDVIEW SURVEY[1]

Every person approaches life with a set of presuppositions by which (s)he sorts out what is meaningful. This is called a World View. Please choose the phrase or statement from the following, which is the closest to how you think or believe.
MORE THAN ONE ANSWER IS ACCEPTABLE

1. ETHICS

a. Morality is relative to each individual & situation; therefore, whatever works best or seems right at the time is the right thing to do.

b. There are no absolute standards; therefore, each person develops their own moral standard.

c. There is a set of absolute moral guidelines established by God that applies to all cultures and times.

d. All moral abuses result from being out of harmony with nature.

e. Morality is meaningless.

f. None of the above.

2. HUMAN SIGNIFICANCE

a. I have significance and dignity specifically because I am made in the image of God.

b. I create my own significance in spite of the fact that there is no ultimate meaning or purpose.

c. I am significant because I am a human being, one of the most highly evolved forms of life on earth.

d. I am significant because of the God-like potential within myself.

e. As a product of directionless evolution, I have no more significance than a rock or a snail.

f. None of the above.

3. A HUMAN IS...

a. A higher animal; the grand result of millions of years of evolution and his/her immediate social upbringing.

b. A being who is incapable of moral perfection and who is therefore in need of God's forgiveness.

c. A being who has the capacity to create meaning and moral values for him/herself and then to live by them.

d. A spiritual being who should look within themselves for divine potential.

e. A physical being who is miserable because (s)he asks questions about meaning and purpose.

f. None of the above.

4. IN YOUR OPINION WHAT HAPPENS TO A PERSON AT DEATH?

a. They cease to exist.

b. They are judged and then rewarded or punished in an after-life according to their choices/actions in this life.

c. They come back in another form (reincarnation), OR pass from one state of illusion to the other.

d. None of the above.

5. THE BEST WAY TO FIND TRUTH IS...

a. Through experimentation on data observable through the five senses.

b. Through mystical experience (Yoga, meditation, visualization, chanting, astral projection, etc.).

c. Through not only the senses & reason but especially through special revelation from God (Holy Scriptures, etc.).

d. God reveals truth only through the senses and reason, not through special, supernatural revelation.

e. Truth is subjective; it is whatever I decide it to be.

f. Because our brains & senses are the products of directionless evolution, we cannot trust our own perceptions of reality; thus, the concept of truth is meaningless.

g. None of the above.

6. GOD IS...

a. The Creator of the universe. He has concern for and is closely involved with his creation, especially human beings.

b. A being who designed the universe and "set it in motion" but who remains uninvolved or, at best, a distant observer.

c. Non-existent.

d. God exists in the minds of some individuals only for the purpose of creating meaning and value.

e. There is an impersonal divine force that exists within everything and everyone.

f. None of the above.

7. Role of Education...

a. One of education's main purposes is to teach tolerance and acceptance of other cultures and world philosophies regardless of their nature.

b. Education is the only source of knowledge that brings success.

c. Religious ideas or opinions have no place in the educational arena.

d. It is acceptable to integrate religion into education; but only if it is taught within a historical context.

e. Educators are responsible for imparting knowledge and practical wisdom including God honoring principles.

f. None of the above.

8. Philosophy...

a. All roads lead to God.

b. The devil does not exist.

c. Jesus is the only source of peace, love, joy, and salvation.

d. Salvation is earned by doing good deeds.

e. The Bible is a book written by mere men and is therefore not the Word of God.

f. None of the above.

Appendix C
Worldview Studies Glossary

The following is a concise list of terms[1] that the writer has deemed necessary for effectiveness in developing and presenting a Christian worldview.

Academic Skepticism[2]: Also known, as the Middle Academy, this term describes an ancient Greek philosophical school. Skepticism is the philosophical attitude of doubting the knowledge claims set forth in various areas and asking what they are based upon, what they actually establish, and whether they are indubitable or necessarily true. Skepticism was first developed in Plato's Academy in Greece in the 3rd century BC; the Academics argued that nothing could be known, and that only reasonable or probable standards could be established for knowledge. Academic Skepticism survived into the Middle Ages in Europe and was considered and refuted by St. Augustine, whose conversion to Christianity convinced him that faith could lead to understanding.

Accommodation: Speaks of God making Himself known to humans in words and ways suitable for the finite human mind to comprehend. The most significant example in which God accommodates to humankind is found in the coming of Jesus Christ-deity taking human form. *See also* incarnation

Adiaphora: Items of belief not essential to salvation. In Lutheran thought the adiaphora were defined as practices of the church that were neither commanded nor forbidden in Scripture.

Adoption: God's act of making otherwise estranged human beings part of God's spiritual family by including them as inheritors of the riches of the divine glory. This adoption takes place through our receiving in faith the work of Jesus Christ the Son (John 3:16), being born of the Spirit (John 3:5-6) and receiving the Spirit of adoption (Romans 8:15-16). See also reconciliation.

Agnosticism: Literally, "no knowledge" taken from two Greek terms, *a* (no) and *gnosis* (knowledge). In a more formal sense *agnosticism* refers to a system of belief in which personal opinion about religious statements (e.g., "God exists") is suspended because it is assumed that they can be neither proven nor disproven or because such statements are seen as irrelevant. *See also* Atheism.

Anthropology: From the Greek words *anthrōpos* (human) and *logos* (word), that is, words about or teaching concerning, human-kind. Anthropology in general refers to any study of the status, habits, customs, relationships and culture of humankind. In a more specific and theological sense, anthropology sets forth the scriptural teachings about humans as God's creatures. Christian anthropology recognizes that humans are created in God's image (**imago Dei*) but that sin has in some way negatively affected that image. Anthropology is also interested in the question of the constitution of a human being, that is, the relationship between body, soul, spirit and so on.

Apologetics: Occasionally called *eristics*, apologetics is the formal defense of the Christian faith. Historically, Christian theologians have differed as to whether apologetics is appropriate to the presentation of the gospel, and if so, how it should be accomplished. Depending on how they have answered these questions, apologists have appealed to rational argumentation, empirical evidence, fulfilled prophecy, authorities of the church or mystical experience in defending such beliefs as the existence of God, the authority of Scripture, the deity of Christ, and the historicity of Jesus' resurrection.

Asceticism: The teaching that spirituality is attained through renunciation of physical pleasures and personal desires while concentrating on "spiritual" matters. Jesus himself advocated certain practices such as fasting (Matthew 9:15) or, for perhaps, celibacy (Matthew 19:12) for the sake of the kingdom; yet some Christians have overemphasized the role of ascetic practices. This prompted the apostle Paul to assert that ascetic practice alone is insufficient as a means of escaping from sin (see Col 2:20-23). Unfortunately, asceticism often proceeds on the assumption that the physical body is evil and is ultimately the cause of sin—a wholly unbiblical concept. *See also* Gnosticism.

Atheism: A system of belief that asserts categorically that there is no God. Atheism also affirms that the only form of existence is the material universe and that man/matter is merely the product of chance or fate. *See also* agnosticism.

Atonement: *Atonement* refers to God's act of dealing with the primary human problem, sin. Both the OT and NT affirm that sin has broken the relationship between God and humankind. According to Christian theology, God accomplished the way of salvation through Christ's death. Although Scripture does not clearly spell out how this atonement takes place, some of the atonement theories include: (1) * moral influence— Christ's death acts as a positive example of love in action; (2) * ransom (*Christus victor*)—Christ is the ransom that buys back sinners from satan or gains the victory over evil; (3) *satisfaction— Christ's death appeased the honor due God that has been robbed by human sin; and (4) *penal substitution—Christ stood in the legal place of sinners, bearing the just punishment due us because we transgress God's laws.

Attribute, attributes of God: In general, an attribute is a characteristic or quality used to describe an object or person. When speaking of the attributes of God, theologians note those characteristics or qualities that are essential to our understanding of God as God relates to us as created beings. The attributes that classical Christian theology sets forth include holiness, eternality, omniscience (all knowing), omnipotence (all powerful), omnipresence (present to all), and goodness. Some theologians would argue that love is an attribute of God, while others suggest is more closely related to God's essential being.

Blessed hope: The biblical phrase used to refer to the second coming of Christ as the fulfillment of our longings (see Titus 2:13). The main twentieth-century evangelical-fundamentalist debate surrounding the blessed hope is whether Christ's appearance will be a secret appearing only to Christians prior to a period of great tribulation (the rapture anticipated by dispensational pretribulational premillennialism) or whether Christ's appearance will be a public event observable by all people, whether Christian or not (most other eschatological positions, including amillennialism, post-millennialism and historic premillennialism).

Causality: A term derived from closely related ideas of cause and effect. In theology, causality as a method seeks to determine the nature and attributes of God by seeking to identify and understand effects present in the world that are assumed to have been caused by God. In short, the method of causality assumes that there are marks left in creation that point out to the ultimate cause, God as Creator.

Christian Manifesto[3]: In this explosive book, Francis Schaeffer shows why morality and freedom have crumbled in our society. He calls for a massive movement—in government, law, and all of life—to reestablish our Judeo- Christian foundation and turn the tide of moral decadence and loss of freedom.

Christian[4]: an adherent or follower of Christ. The word occurs three times in the New Testament: "The disciples were first called Christians in Antioch" (Acts 11:26); Agrippa said to Paul, "You almost persuade me to be a Christian" (Acts 26:28); Peter exhorted, "If anyone suffers as a Christian, let him not be ashamed" (I Peter 4:16). In each instance, the word Christian assumes that the person called by the name was a follower of Christ. Christians were loyal to Christ, just as the Herodians were loyal to Herod (Matthew 22:16; Mark 3:6; 12:13).

The designation of the early followers of Christ as Christians was initiated by the non-Christian population of Antioch. Originally it may have been a term of derision. Eventually, however, Christians used it of themselves as a name of honor, not of shame. Prior to their adoption of the name, the Christians called themselves believers (Acts 9:13), a name that also continued to be used.

Christianity[5]: The Christian religion (faith), which is based on Jesus Christ, the only Savior and Mediator between God the father and sinful man. It is founded on a personal relationship established through reconciliation to God the Father by the atoning death of the Savior. Christianity is unique among all religions of the world. Most religions emphasized the life of their founder, but Christianity is based on the death of Jesus Christ. The death of Jesus is unique as it was prophesied in the opening pages of the Bible (Genesis 3:15) and came to pass in the New Testament age thousand of years later.

Cosmology: Derived from the Greek word *Kosmos* (world), *cosmology* refers to the attempt to understand the origin, nature and subsequent history of the universe. Cosmology and science intersect, insofar as both are interested in understanding whether or not there is a first cause to the universe and whether or not there is purposeful direction and design in the universe.

Culture: n. (from the Latin *cultura* stemming from *colere*, meaning "to cultivate"), generally refers to patterns of human activity and the symbolic structures that give such activity significance. According to the American Heritage College Dictionary, *culture* refers to the totality of socially transmitted behavior patterns, arts, beliefs, institutions, and all other products of human work or thought.

Deism: The belief that understands God as distant, in that God created the universe but then left it to run its course on its own, following certain "laws of nature" that God had built into the universe. An analogy often used to illustrate the deist view is that the artisan, who creates a mechanical clock, winds it up and then leaves the clock alone to "run out." Deism is the belief that God exists, but does not interfere with His creation in any way.

Ethics: The area of philosophical and theological inquiry into what constitutes right and wrong, that is, morality, as well as what is good and the good life. Ethics seeks to provide insight, principles or even a system of guidance in the quest of the good life or in acting rightly in either general or specific situations in life. Broadly speaking, ethical systems are either deontological (seeking to guide behavior through establishment or discovery of what is intrinsically right or wrong) or teleological (seeking to guide behavior through an understanding of the outcomes or ends that ethical decisions and behavior bring about).

Faith: A biblical word refers both to intellectual belief and to relational trust or commitment. The biblical authors generally do not make a distinction between faith as belief and faith as trust, but tend to see true faith as consisting of what is believed (e.g., that God exists, that Jesus is Lord) and the personal commitment to a person who is trustworthy, reliable and able to save (that is, trust in the person of Christ as the way to salvation).

General Revelation: A term used to declare that God reveals something about the divine nature through created order. This self-revealing of God through creation is called general because it only gives "general" or "indirect" information about God, including the fact of God's existence and that God is powerful. This is in contrast to special revelation, which is more "specific" and "direct," and includes the appearance of the living Word (Jesus Christ Himself) and the written Word of God (the Scriptures), revealing a holy, loving and just God who graciously provides forgiveness of sin. General revelation is likewise "general" in that it is available to all humankind, in contrast to the divine self-disclosure that God revealed to certain persons. *See also* special revelation.

Gnosticism: An early Greek religious movement of broad proportions that was particularly influential in the second-century church. Many biblical interpreters see in certain NT documents (such as I John) the attempt to answer or refute Gnostic teaching. The word *gnosticism* comes from the Greek term *gnosis*, meaning "knowledge." Gnostics believed that devotees had gained a special kind of spiritual enlightenment, through which they had attained a secret or higher level of knowledge not accessible to the uninitiated. Gnostics also tended to emphasize the spiritual realm over the material, often claiming that the material realm is evil and hence to be escaped.

Gospel: Literally, the "good news." Defined biblically as the life, death, and resurrection of Jesus Christ for the atonement of mankind's sin (I Corinthians 15:1-3).

Grace (*common, efficacious, prevenient*): One of the central concepts of the Scriptures, grace speaks of God's loving actions toward humankind in particular. Grace is the generous overflow of the love of God the Father through the Son Jesus Christ. This love is most clearly demonstrated to humans through God's selfless giving of Jesus to enable people to enter into a loving relationship with God as the Holy Spirit enables them. *Common Grace* speaks of God's extension of favor to all people through providential care, regardless of whether or not they acknowledge and love God. *Efficacious grace* refers to the special application of grace to a person who comes by faith to Christ for salvation. It is the special act of God that brings about the true salvation of a person. *Prevenient grace*, though often thought to be synonymous with common grace, refers more specifically to the Wesleyan idea that God has enabled all people everywhere to respond favorably to the gospel if they so choose.

Humanism (secular humanism): In general, humanism is any movement or ideology that focuses on the worth of the human being. Christian teachings emphasize the fact that humans are created in God's image and as such are creatures of worth or value.

Secular humanism, on the other hand, attempts to see the worth of humans apart from any appeal to God. Thus the secular humanists often suggest that value is completely intrinsic to the individual.

Idealism: Any philosophical system that describes the nature of reality more in terms of spirit or mind than matter or material. Some idealists argue that all reality is the product of a single mind (or *Geist*), namely, the mind of God (Hegelian idealism), while others suggest that the sum total of many minds (Berkeleian idealism). Still others see reality as a hierarchy and deem the abstract realm of thoughts and ideas to be "more real" than the "less real" concrete realm of physical objects and shadows of objects (Platonic idealism).

Incarnation: Fundamentally, *incarnation* is a theological assertion that in Jesus the eternal Word of God appeared in human form (John 1). Many theologians picture the incarnation as the voluntary and humble act of the second person of the Trinity, God the Son, in taking upon Himself full humanity and living and living a truly human life. The orthodox doctrine of the incarnation asserts in taking humanity upon Himself, Christ did not experience a loss of His divine nature in any way but continued to be fully God.

Inerrancy: The idea that Scripture is completely free from error. It is generally agreed by all theologians who use the term that *inerrancy* at least refers to the trustworthy and authoritative nature of Scriptures as God's Word, which informs humankind of the need for and the way to salvation. Some theologians, however, affirm that the Bible is completely accurate about other subjects, such as science and history.

Infallibility: The characteristic of being incapable of failing to accomplish a predetermined purpose. In Protestant Theology infallibility is usually associated with Scripture. The Bible will not fail in its ultimate purpose of revealing God and the way of salvation to humans.

Justice: In a general sense, the practice of giving reward or punishment for what is rightly due to a person or group of people. From a theological perspective, because God is sinless and holy, the justice of God demands that all persons and nations receive punishment because of their sin. In Christ the requirements of divine justice are met, and as a result, individuals can find mercy from God through Jesus Christ as the Holy Spirit draws them and convicts them of sin. In light of God's own just dealings with humankind, God also demands that humans deal justly with one another (Matthew 23:33) and seek to release those under oppression, whether because of ethnic origin, gender or socio-political status (Isaiah 58:6).

Kingdom: The dynamic reign of God as sovereign over creation. Although the roots of the term lie in the OT, the Christian under-standing arises more specifically from Jesus' proclamation of the inbreaking of God's rule. Hence the kingdom is God's divine, kingly reign as proclaimed and inaugurated by Jesus' life, ministry, death, and resurrection, and the subsequent outpouring of the Holy Spirit into the world. In this sense Christ is reigning now, and the kingdom of God has arrived. At the same time the Church awaits the future consummation of the divine reign. This "already" and "not yet" dimension of the kingdom of God implies that it is both a given reality (or divine power at work in the present) and a process that is moving toward it future fulfill-ment or completion.

Liberalism[6]: A movement in nineteenth- and twentieth-century Protestant movement that favored free intellectual inquiry, stressed the ethical and humanitarian content of Christianity, and de-emphasized dogmatic theology.

Monotheism: The belief in one God (*mono-theos*) as opposed to belief in many gods (polytheism). Although monotheists may acknowledge the reality of other supernatural powers (such as angels and demons), they believe that all such powers are ulti-mately under the control or authority of the one God who alone is supreme. Monotheism in its various forms is found in the teachings of Judaism, Christianity and Islam.

Naturalism (*Natural Theology*): *Naturalism* sometimes refers to a form of atheism and materialism that maintains that the "natural" universe (composed of energy and matter and based on natural laws) is the sum total of reality, thereby negating human freedom, absolute values and, ultimately, existential meaning. As an ethical theory naturalism suggests that ethical judgments arise out of or are based in the universe itself or "the way things naturally are." Natural theology maintains that humans can attain particular knowledge about God through human reason by observing the created order as one locus of divine revelation. Dr. R. C. Sproul[7] refers to *natural theology*, as the "discourse about God informed by our knowledge of nature. It is a knowledge of God gained through an understanding of the external world, in addition to and distinct from the knowledge of God available to us in the Holy Scriptures."

Pantheism: Greek for "everything is God," the belief that God and the universe are essentially identical. More specifically, *pantheism* is the designation for the understanding of the close connection between the world and the divine reality found in certain religions, including Hinduism. One variety of pantheism speaks of God as the "soul" of the universe, which is thought to be God's "body." Pantheistic religions often suggest that our experience of being disconnected from each other and from the divine is merely an illusion.

Pluralism: The advocacy and embrace of a social system that promotes the autonomy and ongoing development of diverse religious, ethnic, racial and social groups within the system. In theology, pluralism suggests that there are many paths to and expression of truth about God and several equally valid means to salvation.

Post-modernism: A term used to designate a variety of intellectual and cultural developments in late-twentieth-century Western society. The postmodern ethos is characterized by a rejection of modernist values and mistrust of the supposedly universal rational principles developed in the enlightenment era. Post-moderns generally embrace pluralism and place value in the diversity of worldviews and religions that characterizes contemporary society.

Presuppositionalism: A variety of classical evangelical apologetics often associated with Cornelius Van Til. Presuppositionalists assert that any system of belief is built on certain foundational presuppositions (unprovable assertions that must be believed to make experience meaningful). As a result, the best means of Christian apologetics is not to prove certain specific assertions such as the existence of God, the historicity of the resurrection or the authority of the Bible. Instead the presuppositionalist Christian apologist explores the foundational presuppositions of competing belief systems with the goal of showing that human experience makes sense (or has meaning) most clearly when viewed in the light of the foundational teachings of the Christian faith. Dr. Norman L. Geisler[8] said, "there is no other way to make sense out of experience except by this presupposition."

Reconciliation: A change in relationship or attitude from enmity to peace; the cessation of hostility in attitude or action. Reconciliation is a central doctrine of Christianity. Specifically, in Christ God reconciled the sinful, hostile world to Himself by Christ's taking upon Himself the cost of our hostility and enmity, thereby setting the world free to restored union with God (II Corinthians 5:19). The foundational assumption of the gospel is that only God can bear the resulting separation from God; therefore God alone can effect this change in relationship.

Relativism: The theory that denies that humans can possess any objective, universally meaningful knowledge, that there are any ultimate and unchanging metaphysical realities (God, persons, space, time, natural laws) or that there are any moral absolutes. Hence meaning and truth are relative to each culture and historical period or to each person, situation, relationship and outcome.

Religion: According to Josh McDowell and Don Stewart[9], religion is that aspect of one's experience in which he attempts to live harmoniously with the power or powers he believes are controlling the world.

Revelation: Refers both to the process by which God discloses the divine nature and the mystery of the divine will and purpose to human beings, and to the corpus of truth disclosed. Some theologians maintain that revelation consists of both God's activity in salvation history through word and deed, culminating in Jesus (who mediates and fulfills God's self-revelation) and the ongoing activity of God to move people to yield to, accept and personally appropriate that reality. General revelation maintains that God's existence and particular attributes can be ascertained through an innate sense of God's reality and conscience as well as through observation of the universe and history. Special revelation refers to the more specific divine self-disclosure to and through certain persons that brings about human salvation.

Secularism, Secular Humanism: Derived from a word that means simply "belonging to this age," or "worldly," secularism is more specifically the belief system that denies the reality of God, religion and the supernatural order and hence maintains that reality entails only this natural world. Secular humanism in turn promotes the human creature to the exclusion and denial of the Creator.

Special Revelation: God's divine self-revelation evidenced specifically in salvation history and culminating in the incarnation as understood through Scripture. Although the Bible seemingly affirms both general and special revelation (*see* revelation), only special revelation can disclose completely our sinful predicament, as well as God's promise of salvation and its fulfillment in Christ.

Spirituality, Christian: The believer's relationship with God and life in the Spirit as a member of the church of Jesus Christ (universal church). Today spirituality often refers to an interest in or concern for matters of the "spirit" in contrast to the mere interest and focus on the material. Christian spirituality in turn entails a desire to allow one's Christian commitment to shape every dimension of life. Some see Christian spirituality as expressed through participation in certain Christian practices, such as Bible study, prayer, worship and so forth.

Theism: The system of belief that presupposes the reality of God as the foundational concept informing all other beliefs. Any worldview anchored in the belief that there is a God.

Truth: That which reflects factual and/or spiritual reality. Some thinkers view truth in purely intellectual categories, namely, as the affirmation of what is. Hence truth becomes correct assertions or factual statements (factuality). In recent times certain thinkers have suggested that truth is subjective, relative and pluralistic. Viewed from a theological perspective, truth is grounded in the being and will of triune God. Hence whatever reflects God's own being and will is truth. Furthermore, Jesus Christ is the truth in that he is the revelation of God.

Worldview (Weltanschauung)[10]: [from German *Welt,* world (< MHGer. *wërlt* < OHGer. *Weralt*; see). A comprehensive philosophy of the world or of human life. Thus, a worldview is a collection of beliefs about life and the universe held by an individual or a group.

NOTES

Appendix B

[1] Adapted from a worldview survey instrument written by David Montsya, *The Worldview Computer Survey: An Interactive, Evangelistic Survey.* Roseville, CA: Montoya, 1993. Source: Retrieved on March 25, 2003 from http://www.student.nada.kth.se/~d93-tol/worldview/
Other sources that use the same survey include: Philip Billington and from UCCF (Universities and Colleges Christian Fellowship), which is made up of Christian Unions (CUs) in England, Scotland and Wales.

Appendix C

[1] Most of the terms outlined in this section (unless otherwise mentioned) are taken from the following: Evans, C. Stephen, *Pocket Dictionary of Apologetics & Philosophy.* (Downers Grove, IL: Intervarsity Press, 2002).
Stanley J. Grentz, David Guretzki and Cherith Fee Nordling, *Pocket Dictionary of Theological Terms.* (Downers Grove, IL: Intervarsity Press, 1999).
Josh McDowell and Don Stewart, *Handbook of Today's Religions.* (Nashville, TN: Thomas Nelson Publishers, 1983).
[2] American Heritage, *The American Heritage College Dictionary* (3rd ed.). (Boston, MA: Houghton Mifflin Company, 1997), 1276.

[3] Francis A. Schaffer, *A Christian Manifesto.* (Wheaton, IL: Crossway Books, 1981), back cover.

[4] Herbert Locker(Ed), *The Illustrated Dictionary of the Bible.* (Nashville, TN: Thomas Nelson Publishers, 1986), 219.

[5] Ibid. 220.

[6]American Heritage, *The American Heritage College Dictionary* (3rd ed.). (Boston, MA: Houghton Mifflin Company, 1997), 781.

[7]R.C. Sproul, *Defending Your Faith: An Introduction to Apologetics.* (Wheaton, Il: Crossway Books, 2003), 74.

[8]Norman L. Geisler, *Christian Apologetics.* (Grand Rapids, MI: Baker Book House Company, 1976), 125.

[9]Josh McDowell and Don Stewart, *Handbook of Today's Religions.* (Nashville, TN: Thomas Nelson Publishers, 1983), 11.

[0]American Heritage, *The American Heritage College Dictionary* (3rd ed.). (Boston, MA: Houghton Mifflin Company, 1997), 1532 and 1555.

NOTES

—〜〜—

Introduction

[1] Barna Research Group, *A Biblical Worldview Has a Radical Effect on a Person's Life.* Ventura, CA: Barna Update (December 1, 2003). Retrieved on December 15, 2008 from http://www.barna. org/FlexPage.aspx?Page=BarnaUpdate&BarnaUpdateID=154.

[2] Ronald H. Nash, *The Christian Parent and Student Guide to Choosing a College.* (Brentwood, TN: Wolgemuth & Hyatt Publishers, 1989), 3.

Chapter One

[1] Blaise Pascal. *Pensées.* Translated by A. J. Krailsheimer. (London: Penguin, 1966), #148, 75.

[2] Robert L. Sidmonds, *Religion and Culture in History: Teacher Guidelines for Teaching the Christian/ American Culture.* (San Diego, CA: A Unit in Multicultural Curriculum, The California History-Social Science Project at the University of California, n.d.). Retrieved on November 14, 2003 from http://www.nace-cee.org/ teachingchculture.htm

[3] Robert L. Waggoner, *Biblical Theism vs. Secular Humanism: A Class to Train Theists to Confront Humanism.* (Brentwood, TN: Erskine Theological Seminary, 2000), 11.

[4] The Pew Research Center for the People and the Press. *The Pew Global Attitudes Project: U.S. Stands alone in its Embrace of Religion.* (Washington, D.C.: The Pew Research Center, 2002), 1. Retrieved on December 18, 2008 from http://pewglobal.org/reports/pdf/167.pdf.

[5] Don Closson, *Politically Correct Education.* (Richardson, TX: Probe Ministries, 1992), 1.

[6] Ibid., 4.

[7] Russ Wise, *Education and New Age Humanism.* (Richardson, TX: Probe Ministries, 1995), 2.

[8] Ibid., 2.

Chapter Two

[1] Webster's Revised Unabridged Dictionary (1913), 471.

[2] Ibid., 471.

[3] Pamela J. Farris. *Teaching and Bearing the Torch.* (Boston, MA: Mc Graw-Hill College, 1999), 88-93.

[4] Allan C. Ornstein and Daniel U. Levine. *Foundations of Education.* (Boston: Houghton Mifflin Company, 2000), 392.

[5] Richard D. Mosier, *"Perennialism in Education,"* History of Education Journal 2, no. 3 (Spring, 1951): 80-85.

[6] Pennsylvania State University. Retrieved on May 23, 2008 from "http://www2.yk.psu.edu/~jlg18/506/Word%20files/philosophy/Perennialism_reading.doc."

[7] Mortimer J. Adler, *The Paideia Proposal: An Educational Manifesto.* (New York, NY: Mcmillan Publishing Company, 1982), 69-70.

[8] David E. Denton, "Existentialism in American Educational Philosophy," *International Review of Education/ International Zeitschrift fürErziehungswissenschaft/ Revue Internationale de l'Éducation,* 14, No.1 , (1968):100-101. Retrieved on May 20, 2007 from http://www.jstor.org/stable/pdfplus/3442112.pdf

[9] Taken from George R. Knight. *Philosophy & Education: an Introduction in Christian Education.* (Berrien Springs, MI: Andrews University Press, 1998), 79.

[10] Myra Pollack Sadker and David Miller Sadker, *Teachers, Schools, and Society* (New York, NY: McGraw Hill Higher Education, 2005), 345.

[11] Internet Encyclopedia of Philosophy, University of Tennessee at Martin Retrieved on May 7, 2008 from "http://www.iep.utm.edu/d/dewey.htm" University of Tennessee at Martin, Dec 28, 2005.

[12] "My brethren, let not many of you become teachers, knowing that we shall receive a stricter judgment."

[13] Francis A. Schaffer, *Escape from Reason.* (Downers Grove, IL: Intervarsity Press, 2006 (originally printed in 1968), 17.

[14]These verses have been known in Jewish tradition for centuries as "The Shema," which contains the fundamental truth of Israel's religion. They are recited as a daily prayer along with Deuteronomy 11:13-21 and Numbers 15:37-41.

[15] Kenneth O. Gangel and Warren S. Benson, *Christian Education: Its History and Philosophy.* (Chicago, IL: Moody Press, 1983), 22.

[16] Ibid., 22.

[17] John B. Huslt, "Key Note Address" Christian Worldview and Scholarship, ed. John B. Hulst (Melbourne, Australia: Amani, 2004), 16.

[18] R.C. Sproul, *Defending Your Faith: An Introduction to Apologetics.* (Wheaton, IL: Crossway Publishing, 2003), 7.

[19] Myra Pollack Sadker and David Miller Sadker, *Teachers, Schools, and Society* (New York, NY: McGraw Hill Higher Education, 2005), 285.

[20] Stephen Tchudi and Diana Mitchell, *Exploring and Teaching the English Language Arts* (Reading, MA: Addison Wesley Educational Publishers, Inc., 1999), 5.

[21] Kenneth O. Gangel and Warren S. Benson, *Christian Education: Its History and Philosophy.* (Chicago, IL: Moody Press, 1983), 230.

[22] Ibid., 230.

[23] John R. Thelin, *A History of American Higher Education.* (Baltimore, MD: The John Hopkins University Press, 2004), 23.

[24] Myra Pollack Sadker and David Miller Sadker, *Teachers, Schools, and Society* (New York, NY: McGraw-Hill Higher Education), 289.

[25] John H. Roberts and James Turner, *The Sacred and the Secular University* (Princeton: Princeton University Press, 2000), 20.

[26] Harvard University, About the shield and Logo of Harvard University. Retrieved December 24, 2005, from http://hcs.harvard.edu/~gsascf/shield.html

[27] Kenneth O. Gangel and Warren S. Benson, *Christian Education: Its History and Philosophy.* (Chicago, IL: Moody Press, 1983), 232.

[28] "The general principle in the matter of public education is that anyone is free to found a public school and to direct it as he pleases. It's an industry like other industries, the consumers being the judges and the state taking no hand whatever... There has never been under the sun person as enlightened as the population of the north of the United States." Alexis De Tocqueville, quoted in George W. Pierson (1959). *Tocqueville in America.* (Garden City: Anchor Books), 293-294. "Apart from New England, where tax-supported schools existed under state law, the United States, from 1789 to 1835, had a completely *lassés-faire* system of education.... there were no compulsory attendance laws anywhere. Parents educated their children as they wished.... There was no need for any child to go without an education. The rate of literacy in the United States then was probably higher than it is today." Samuel L. Blumenfield (1985). *Is Public Education Necessary?* (Boise, Idaho: The Paradigm Company), 27.

[29] Robert A. Peterson (1979). *Education in Colonial America.* Cited by Rus Walton (1987). *One Nation Under God.* (Nashville: Thomas Nelson Publishers), 61.

[30] Myra Pollack Sadker and David Miller Sadker, *Teachers, Schools, and Society* (New York, NY: McGraw-Hill Higher Education), 289.

Chapter Three

[1] C.S. Lewis, "hearing in War-time," *In the Weight of Glory* (San Francisco: HarperSanFrancisco, 1980), 59.

[2] Florida State University, *"What is Philosophy?"* Retrieved May 7, 2007 from "http://www.fsu.edu/~philo/new%20site/sub_category/whatisphilo.htm" What is philosophy?

[3] Josh McDowell and Don Stewart, *Handbook of Today's Religions* (Nashville, TN: Thomas Nelson Reference, 1992), 11.

[4] From Sir Norman Anderson, ed., *The World's Religions*, Grand Rapids, MI: William B. Eerdmans Publishing Company, 1976.

[5] R.C. Sproul, *Lifeviews* (Old Tappan H. Revell, 1986), 29.

[6] Ronald H. Nash, *Faith & Reason* (Grand Rapids, 1988), 26.

[7] William James (1902), *The Varieties of Religious Experience.* (New York: Longman), p. 53.

[8] Bruce Bickel and Stan Jantz, World *Religions and Cults 101: A Guide to Spiritual beliefs.* (Eugene, Oregon: Harvest House Publishers, 2002), p. 7.

[9] Sigmund Freud, *Civilization and its Discontent*, trans ed. James Strachey (New York: W.W. Norton, 1961), 19.

[10] In psychoanalysis, a subconscious sexual desire in a child, esp. a male child, for the parent of the opposite sex, this may result in neurosis in adulthood.

[11] Ravi Zacharias, *Can Man Live without God.* (Nashville, TN: Word Publishing Group, a Division of Thomas Nelson, 1994), 121.

[12] R.C. Sproul, *Defending your Faith: An Introduction to Apologetics.* (Wheaton, IL: Crossway Books, 2003), 158.

[13] Stephen C. Rockeffeler, *John Dewey: Religious Faith and Democratic Humanism* (New York: Columbia University Press, 1991), pp. 171-72.

[14] David H. Roper, *"John Dewey: A History of Religious Education,* ed. Elmer L. Towns (Grand Rapids: Baker Book House, 1975), 315.

[15] Michael J. Anthony, *Introducing Christian Education: Foundations for the Twenty-First Century,* (Grand Rapids, MI: Baker Academic, 2001), 30.

[16] Article based on Dr. Lumm's doctoral dissertation, reprinted from *Balance,* a publication of the School of Education, Bob Jones University.
L. Werner Lumm, *A Biblical Analysis of the Educational Philosophy expressed by John Dewey in his Original Writings.* Unpublished Dissertation, (Greenville, SC: Bob Jones University, 1996).

[17] Robert W. Pazmiño, *Foundational Issues in Christian Education* (Grand Rapids, MI: Baker Book House Company, 1997), 155.

[18] The best introduction to Dewey's educational thought is provided in Martin S. Dworkin, *Dewey on Education: Selections with an Introduction and Notes* (New York: Teachers College Press, 1959).
From a Christian perspective, Dewey must first be criticized for his ahistorical pragmaticism and presentism. Christianity is a historical faith. Second, Dewey must be criticized for his anti-supernatural bias that discounts the place of revelation. Christianity is revealed faith (religion). Third, Dewey must be criticized for his faith in progress and education and for his assumption that education can result in the salvation of persons. Christianity maintains the reality of sin and that salvation comes through faith in Jesus Christ by the grace of God. Beyond these criticisms, much can gained from a study of Dewey.

[19] Ronald H. Nash, *The Christian Parent and Student Guide to choosing a College* (Brentwood, TN: Wolgemuth & Hyatt, 1989), 90.

[20] James Davison Hunter, *Evangelicalism, The Coming Generation* (Chicago: University of Chicago Press, 1987), 172.

[21] Jeff Astley, Leslie J Francis and Colin Crowder (editors), *Theological Perspectives on Christian Formation: A Reader on Theology and Christian Education*, (Grand Rapids, MI: W. B. Eerdmans Publishing Company, 1996), 117.

[22] John MacArthur (General Editor) with the Master's College Faculty, *Think Biblically! Recovering a Christian Worldview*, (Wheaton, IL: Crossway Books, 2003), 245.

[23] Alfred North Whitehead, *The Rhythm of Education, The Aims of Education* and Other Essays. (New York, NY: The Free Press, 1967), chapter 2.

[24] Decker F. Walker, and Jonas F. Soltis, *Curriculum and Aims*. (New York, NY: Teachers College Press, 1986), 34-35.

Chapter Four

[1] Benjamin B. Warfield, *The Religious Life of Theological Student*, (Phillipsburg, NJ: P.& R Publishing, 1992), 4.

[2] This four-fold purpose I specifically outline in the biblical text to be teaching, to bring conviction, to make correction and to train the hearers to live a righteous life: a purpose that James later outlined in his epistle when he said that we ought to "be doers of the Word, and not hearers only, deceiving ourselves." (James 1:22)

[3] Ronald Nash, *The Myth of a value-Free Education*, (Grand Rapids, MI: Acton Institute, 2004), 1. Source: http://www.acton.org/publicat/randl/article.php?id=18

[4] Jeff Astley, Leslie J Francis and Colin Crowder (editors), *Theological Perspectives on Christian Formation: A Reader on*

Theology and Christian Education, (Grand Rapids, MI: W. B. Eerdmans Publishing Company, 1996), 103.

[5] Ibid., 1.

[6] Back cover of George M. Marsden's book, *The Soul of the American University: from Protestant Establishment to Established Nonbelief* (Oxford, UK: Oxford University Press, 1994).

[7] Francis A. Schaffer, *A Christian Manifesto.* (Wheaton, IL: Crossway Books, 1981), 46-47.

Chapter Five

[1] C. S. Lewis, *A Christian Manifesto.* (Wheaton, IL: Crossway Books, 1981), 17-18.

Chapter Six

[1] Pamela J. Farris, *Teaching, Bearing the Torch.* (Boston, MA: McGraw-Hill College, 1999), 34.

[2] Allan C. Ornstein and Daniel U. Levine, *Foundations of Education.* (Boston, MA: Houghton Mifflin Company, 2000), 453.

[3] John S. Park and Gayle D. Beebe (Editors), *Religion and Its Relevance in Post-Modernism: Essays in honor of Jack C. Verheyden.* (Lewiston, NY: The Edwin Mellen Press, 2001), 77.

[4] Darwin K. Glassford, *Toward a Theological Foundation for Christian Higher Education*, 1. Retrieved on June 6, 2003 from http://capo.org/premise/96/mj/p960507.html.

[5] Charles Colson and Nancy Pearcy, *How now shall we live?* (Wheaton, IL: Tyndale House Publishers, 2001), 22.

[6] Part of this text was adopted from a paper written by my wife, Marsha Valmyr on "*Modernism, Postmodernism and Post-colonialism*" for a graduate English course, entitled Voices in Twentieth Century British literature, dated from February, 2006.

[7] E.J. Barton and G.A. Hudson, *A Contemporary Guide to Literary Terms*. (New York: Houghton Mifflin Company, 1997), 122.

[8] M.H. Abrams, et al. (Eds.) *The Norton Anthology of English literature*, Volume 2 (7th ed.). (New York: W.W. Norton & Company, 2000), 1902.

[9] Ibid, 1946.

[10] Ibid, 2188.

[11] Ibid, 2173.

[12] R. Wesley Hurd, *Postmoderninsm* Article quoted from *McKenzie Study Center*; an institute of Gutenberg College. Retrieved on April 23, 2007 from http://www.mckenziestudycenter.org/philosophy/articles/postmod.html

[13] E.J. Barton and G.A. Hudson, *A Contemporary Guide to Literary Terms*. (New York: Houghton Mifflin Company, 1997), 166.

[14] Jeanette Wintersen, *Oranges are not the only fruit*. (New York: The Atlantic Monthly Press, 1985), 3.

[15] Ibid, 29.

[16] Ibid, 93.

[17] E.J. Barton and G.A. Hudson, *A Contemporary Guide to Literary Terms*. (New York: Houghton Mifflin Company, 1997),166.

[18] Ché Ahn and Lou Engle, *The Call Revolution: A Radical Invitation to Turn the Heart of a Nation back to God.* (Colorado Springs, CO: Wagner Publications, 2001), 32.

[19] David F. Dawes. *Design or Chance.* Article quoted from *Faith Today*, (January/February 2004); an online magazine published by the Evangelical Fellowship of Canada. Retrieved July 28, 2006 from http://www.faithtoday.ca/article_viewer.asp? *Article_ID=109.*

[20] John MacArthur (General editor) and Richard Mayhue. *Think Biblically: Recovering a Christian Worldview.* (Wheaton, IL: Crossway Books, 2003), 221.

[21] Ibid, 221.

[22] Taken from an article entitled *Science, Postmodernism, and Philosophy* by Warren Murray. Alice Ramos and Marie I. George (editors). *Faith, Scholarship, and Culture in the 21st Century.* (Washington, D.C.: American Maritain Association, 2002), 129.

[23] Ibid, 129.

[24] Henry M. Morris. *Science and the Bible (Revised and Updated).* (Chicago, IL.: Moody Press, 186), 44-45.

[25] John MacArthur (General editor) and Richard Mayhue. *Think Biblically: Recovering a Christian Worldview.* (Wheaton, IL: Crossway Books, 2003), 209.

[26] Gary R. Collins. *Christian Counseling: A Comprehensive Guide.* (Nashville, TN: W. Publishing Group, 1988), 22.

[27] Taken from an article entitled *Why Biblical Counseling and Not Psychology* by John D. Street. John MacArthur (General editor) and Richard Mayhue. *Think Biblically: Recovering a Christian Worldview.* (Wheaton, IL: Crossway Books, 2003), 204.

[28] R.C. Sproul, *Defending Your Faith: An Introduction to Apologetics.* (Wheaton, IL: Crossway Publishing, 2003), 159.

[29] John MacArthur, *The Vanishing Conscience.* (Dallas, TX: Word Publishing, 1994), 21.

Chapter Seven

[1] Charles Colson and Nancy Pearcey. *How Now Shall We Live?* (Wheaton, IL: Tyndale House Publishers, 1999), 310-311.

[2] Taken from the article first printed in the National Review, December 10, 1982 Educational Excellence Network Vol. II, No. 4. March, 1983. Reprinted in Network News & Views Vol. XV, No. 12 December 1996.

[3] George M. Marsden, *The Soul of the American University: From Protestant Establishment to Established Nonbelief.* (Oxford, UK: Oxford University Press, 1994), 297.

Chapter Eight

[1] Ronald H. Nash, *Worldviews in Conflicts: Choosing Christianity in a World of Ideas.* (Grand Rapids, MI: Zondervan Publishing House, 1992), 16.

[2] Harry Lee Poe, *Christianity in the Academy: Teaching at the Intersection of Faith and Learning.* (Grand Rapids, MI: Baker Academics, 2004), 21.

Chapter Nine

[1] Wilbert J. McKeachie and Marilla Svinicki, *McKeachie's Teaching Tips: Strategies, Research, and Theory for College and University Teachers.* (Boston, MA: Houghton Mifflin Company, 2006), 57.

[2] Ibid, 58.

[3] Intelligence theorists fall into two categories. In one group are those who argue for a "general intelligence," a single, general aptitude or ability. In the other are those who believe that intelligence is composed of many separate and distinct aptitude or abilities. Taken from Morris, Charles G. and Albert A. Maisto. *Psychology an Introduction (Eleventh Edition)*. (Upper Saddle River, NJ: Prentice Hall, 2002), 346.

[4] Taken from Ken Smitherman, *Shaping a Worldview.* Christian School Comment Vol.38, Num. 2 (Colorado Springs, CO: Association Christian Schools International).

[5] Plato. *The Republic of Plato (Second Edition):Translated with Notes, and an Interpretive Essay and a New Introduction by Allan David Bloom.* (New York, NY: Basic Books, 1991), (518b-c)197.

[6] Bruce A. Little, *Christian Education, Worldviews, and Postmodernity's Challenge.* (Lynchburg, VA: Journal of the Evangelical Theological Society, 1997, accessed March 15, 2006); available from http://www.etsjets.org/jets/journal/40/40-3/40-3-pp433-444_JETS.pdf

Chapter Ten

[1] Chip Ingram, *Good to Great in God's Eyes.* (Grand Rapids, MI: BakerBooks, 2007), 35-52.

BIBLIOGRAPHY

—⁓—

Abrahams, M. H. et al. (Eds.). *The Norton Anthology to English Literature, Volume 2 (7th ed.).* New York, NY: W. W. Norton & Company, 2000.

Ahn, Ché and Lou Engle. *The Call Revolution: A Radical Invitation to Turn the Heart of a Nation Back to God.* Colorado Springs: Wagner Publishers, 2001.

Anderson, Norman. *The World's Religions.* Grand Rapids, MI: William B. Eerdmans Publishing Company, 1976.

Anthony, Michael J. *Introduction to Christian Education: Foundations for the Twenty-First Century.* Grand Rapids, MI: Baker Academic, 2001.

Astley, Jeff, Leslie J Francis and Colin Crowder (editors). *Theological Perspectives on Christian Formation: A Reader on Theology and Christian Education.* Grand Rapids, MI: W. B. Eerdmans Publishing Company, 1996.

Barton, David. *A Guide to the School Prayer & Religious Liberty Debate.* Aledo, TX: Rebuilder Press, 1995.

Bickel, Bruce and Stan Jantz. *World Religions & Cults 101: A Guide to Spiritual Beliefs*. Eugene, IL: Harvest House Publishers, 2002.

Barbour, Ian G. *Nature, Human Nature, and God*. Minneapolis: Fortress Press, 2002.

Barton, E. J. and G. A. Hudson. *A Contemporary Guide to Literary Terms*. New York, NY: Houghton Mifflin Company, 1997.

Belzen, J. A. *Hermeneutical Approaches in Psychology of Religion*. Amsterdam, Netherlands: Rodopi BV Editions, 1997.

Berthold Jr., Fred. *God, Evil, and Human Learning: A Critique and Revision of the Free Will Defense Theology*. Albany, NY: State University of New York Press, 2004.

Bloom, Allan. *The Republic of Plato (Second Edition)*. New York, NY: Basic Books, 1991.

_____. *The Closing of the American Mind*. Parsippany, NJ: Simon & Schuster, 1988.

Brown, Stuart. *Philosophy of Religion: An Introduction with Readings*. London, England: Routledge, 2001.

Bush, L. Russ. *A Handbook for Christian Philosophy*. Grand Rapids, MI: Zondervan, 1991.

Closson, Don. *Politically Correct Education*. Richardson, TX: Probe Ministries, 1992.

Collins, Gary R. *Christian Counseling: A Comprehensive Guide*. Nashville, TN: W. Publishing Group, 1988.

Colson, Charles. *Kingdoms in Conflict: An Insider's Challenging View of Politics, Power, and the Pulpit*. New York, NY: Co publication of William Morrow and Zondervan Publishing House, 1987.

Colson, Charles and Nancy Pearson. *How Now shall we Live?* Wheaton, IL: Tyndale House Publishers, 1999.

Copley, Terence. *Teaching Religion: Fifty Years of Religious Education in England and Wales.* Exeter, UK: University of Exeter Press, 1997.

Crawford, Robert. *The God/Man/World Triangle: A Dialogue between Science and Religion.* London: Macmillan Press Ltd., 1997.

Davies, Douglas. *Anthropology Theology.* Oxford, UK: Berg Publishers, 2002.

Dawes, David F. *Design or Chance.* Article quoted from *Faith Today*, (January/February 2004); an online magazine published by the Evangelical Fellowship of Canada. Retrieved July 28, 2006 from http://www.faithtoday.ca/article_viewer. asp?*Article_ID=109*.

Denton, David E. "Existentialism in American Educational Philosophy," *International Review of Education/ International Zeitschrift fürErziehungswissenschaft/ Revue Internationale de l'Éducation,* 14, No.1 , (1968):100-101. Retrieved on May 20, 2007 from http://www.jstor.org/stable/ pdfplus/3442112.pdf

Duncan, Homer. *Secular Humanism: The Most Dangerous Religion in America.* Lubbock, TX: Christian Focus on Government, 1979.

Dworkin, Martin S. *Dewey on Education: Selections.* New York, NY: Teachers College Press, 1959.

Ellens, J. Harold and Wayne G. Rollins. *Psychology and the Bible: A New Way to Read the Scriptures (Vol. 1 From Freud to Kohut).* Westport, CT: Intervarsity Press, 2004.

_____. *Psychology and the Bible: A New Way to Read the Scriptures (Vol. 2 From Genesis to Apocalyptic Vision).* Westport, CT: Intervarsity Press, 2004.

_____. *Psychology and the Bible: A New Way to Read the Scriptures (Vol. 3 From Gospel to Gnostics).* Westport, CT: Intervarsity Press, 2004.

_____. *Psychology and the Bible: A New Way to Read the Scriptures (Vol. 4 From Christ to Jesus).* Westport, CT: Intervarsity Press, 2004.

Evans, C. Stephen. *Pocket Dictionary of Apologetics & Philosophy.* Downers Grove, IL: Intervarsity Press, 2002.

Farris, Pamela J. *Teaching and Bearing the Torch.* Boston, MA: Mac Graw-Hill College, 1999.

Florida State University. *What is Philosophy?* http://www.fsu. edu/~philo/new%20site/sub_category/whatisphilo.htm"

Ford, David F. *Theology: A Very Short Introduction.* Oxford, England: Oxford University Press, 1999.

Freud, Sigmund. *Civilization and its Discontent, Trans. Ed. James Strachery.* New York, NY: W.W. Norton, 1961.

Gangel, Kenneth O. and Warren S. Benson. *Christian Education: Its History and Philosophy.* Chicago, IL: Moody Press, 1983.

Geisler, Norman L. *Christian Apologetics.* Grand Rapids, MI: Baker Book House, 1976.

Glassford, Darwin K. *Toward a Theological Foundation for Christian Higher Education*, 1. Retrieved on June 6, 2003 from http://capo.org/premise/96/mj/p960507.html.

Grentz, Stanley J. and David Gurezki and Cherith Fee Nordlin. *Pocket Dictionary of Theological Terms*. Downers Grove, IL: Intervarsity Press, 1999.

Gunton, Colin E. *The Christian Faith: An Introduction to Christian Doctrine*. Oxford, UK: Blackwell Press, 2002.

Harvard University, About the shield and Logo of Harvard University. Retrieved on December 24, 2005, from http://hcs.harvard. edu/~gsascf/shield.html

Holifield, E. Brooks. *Theology in America: Christian Thought from the Age of the Puritans to the Civil War.* New Haven, CT: Yale University Press, 2003.

Hunter, James Davison. *Evangelicalism, The Coming Generation.* Chicago, IL: University of Chicago Press, 1987.

Hurd, R. Wesley. *Postmoderninsm* Article quoted from *McKenzie Study Center*; an institute of Gutenberg College, 3. Retrieved on April 23, 2007 from http://www.mckenziestudycenter. org/philosophy/articles/postmod.html

Ingram, Chip, *Good to Great in God's Eyes*. Grand Rapids, MI: BakerBooks, 2007.

Internet Encyclopedia of Philosophy, University of Tennessee at Martin Retrieved on May 7, 2008 from "http://www.iep.utm. edu/d/dewey.htm" University of Tennessee at Martin, Dec 28, 2005.

James, Williams. *The Varieties of Religious Experience*. New York, NY: Longman, Green & Co., 1902.

Johnson, James A, Victor L. Dupuis, and Diann Musial. *Introduction to the Foundations of American Education.* Boston: Allyn And Bacon, 2002.

Kennedy, D. James. *Why I Believe.* Waco, TX: Word Books Publisher, 1980.

Kienel, Paul A. *A History of Christian School Education.* Colorado Springs, CO: Association of Christian Schools International, 1998.

Knight, George R. *Philosophy & Education: An Introduction in Christian Education.* Berrien Springs, MI: Andrews University Press, 1998.

Lewis, C.S. *"Hearing in War-Time," In the Weight of Glory.* San Francisco, CA: HarperSan Francisco, 1980.

_____. *Mere Christianity.* New York, NY: HarperCollins Publishers, 2001.

Little, Bruce A. *Christian Education, Worldviews, and Postmodernity's Challenge.* (Lynchburg, VA: Journal of the Evangelical Theological Society, 1997, accessed March 15, 2006); available from http://www.etsjets.org/jets/journal/40/40-3/40-3-pp433-444_JETS.pdf

Locker, Herbert. *The Illustrated Dictionary of the Bible.* Nashville, TN: Thomas Nelson Publishers, 1986.

Lumm, L. Werner. *A Biblical Analysis of the Educational Philosophy expressed by John Dewey in his Original Writings.* Unpublished Dissertation. Greenville, SC: Bob Jones University, 1996.

MacArthur, John. *Think Biblically! Recovering a Christian Worldview.* Wheaton: Crossway Books, Good News Publishers, 2003.

_____ The *Vanishing Conscience.* Dallas, TX: Word Publishing, 1994.

McKeachie, Wilbert J. and Marilla Svinicki (Editors). *McKeachie's Teaching Tips: Strategies, Research, and Theory for College and University Teachers (Twelfth Edition).* Boston, MA: Houghton Mifflin Company, 2006.

Marsden, George M. *The Soul of the American University: From Protestant Establishment to Established Nonbelief.* Oxford: Oxford University Press, 1994.

McDowell, Josh and Don Stewart. *Handbook of Today's Religions.* Nashville: Thomas Nelson Publishers, 1983.

Montsya, David *The Worldview Computer Survey: An Interactive, Evangelistic Survey.* Roseville, CA: Montoya, 1993. Retrieved on March 25, 2003 from http://www.student.nada.kth.se/~d93-tol/worldview/

Morris, Henry M. *Science and the Bible (Revised and Updated).* Chicago: Moody Press, 1986.

Mosier, Richard D. *"Perennialism in Education,"* History of Education Journal 2, no. 3 (Spring, 1951): 80-85.

Nash, Ronald H. *Worldviews in Conflict: Choosing Christianity in a world of ideas.* Grand Rapids: Zondervan Publishing House, 1992.

_____ *Faith and Reason: Searching for a Rational Faith.* Grand Rapids: Zondervan Publishing House, 1988.

_____ *The Myth of a value-Free Education*, (Grand Rapids, MI: Acton Institute, 2004), 1. Source: http://www.acton.org/publicat/randl/article.php?id=18

_____ *The Christian Parent and Student Guide to Choosing a College*. Brentwood, TN: Wolgemuth and Hyatt Publishers, 1989.

Newell, Norman D. *Creation and Evolution*. New York, NY: Columbia University Press, 1982.

Ornstein, Allan C. and Daniel U. Levine. *Foundations of Education*. Boston, MA: Houghton Mifflin Company, 2000.

Park, John S. and Gayle D. Beebe (Editors), *Religion and Its Relevance in Post-Modernism: Essays in honor of Jack C. Verheyden*. Lewiston, NY: The Edwin Mellen Press, 2001.

Pascal, Blaise. *Pensées*. Translated by A. J. Krailsheimer. London: Penguin, 1966.

Pazmiño, Robert W. *Foundational Issues in Christian Education*. Grand Rapids, MI: Baker Book House Company, 1997.

Pearsey, Nancy R. *Total Truth: Liberating Christianity from Its Captivity*. Wheaton, IL: Crossway Books, 2004.

Pennsylvania State University. Retrieved on May 23, 2008 from "http://www2.yk.psu.edu/~jlg18/506/Word%20files/philosophy/Perennialism_reading.doc."

Peterson, Robert A. *Education in Colonial America*. Cited by Rus Walton (1987). *One Nation Under God*. Nashville: Thomas Nelson Publishers, 1979.

Phillips, Gary W. and William E. Brown. *Making Sense of your World from a Biblical Viewpoint*. Chicago: Moody, 1991.

Poe, Harry Lee. *Christianity in the Academy: Teaching at the Intersection of Faith and Learning.* Grand Rapids, MI: Baker Academic, 2004.

Rae, Scott B. *Moral Choices: An Introduction to Ethics, Second Edition.* Grand Rapids, MI: Zondervan Publishing House, 2000.

Ramos, Alice and Marie I. George (editors). *Faith, Scholarship, and Culture in the 21st Century.* Washington, D.C.: American Maritain Association, 2002.

Ratzinger, Joseph Cardinal. *Truth and Tolerance: Christian Belief and World Religions (Translated by Henry Taylor).* San Francisco, CA: Ignatius Press, 2004.

Roberts, Richards H. *Religion, Theology and the Human Sciences.* Cambridge: Cambridge University Press, 2002.

Roberts, John H. and James Turner. *The Sacred and the Secular University.* Princeton, NJ: Princeton University Press, 2000.

Rockeffeler, Stephen C. *John Dewey: Religious Faith and Democratic Humanism.* New York, NY: Columbia University Press, 1991.

Roper, David H. *John Dewey: A History of Religious Education, ed. Elmer Towns.* Grand Rapids, MI: Baker Book House, 1975.

Sadker, Myra Pollack and David Miller Sadker. *Teachers, Schools, and Society.* New York, NY: McGraw Hill Higher Education, 2005.

Saunders, George R. (Editor). *Culture and Christianity: The Dialectics of Transformation.* New York, NY: Greenwood Press, 1998.

Schaeffer, Francis A. *Escape from Reason*. Downers Grove, IL: Intervarsity Press (originally printed in 1968), 2006.

_____. *A Christian Manifesto*. Wheaton, IL: Crossway Books, Good News Publishers, 2005.

_____. *The Rise and Decline of Western Thought and Culture: How Should We Then Live?* Wheaton: Crossway Books, Good News Publishers, 2005.

Schuurman, Douglas J. *Vocation: Discerning our Calling in Life*. Grand Rapids, MI: William. B. Eerdmans Company, 2004.

Sidmonds, Robert L. *Religion and Culture in History: Teacher Guidelines for Teaching the Christian/ American Culture*. San Diego, CA: A Unit in Multicultural Curriculum, The California History-Social Science Project at the University of California, n.d. Retrieved on November 14, 2003 from http://www.nacecee.org/teachingchculture.htm

Smitherman, Ken. *Shaping a Worldview*. Christian School Comment Vol.38, Num. 2 Colorado Springs, CO: Association Christian Schools International.

Sowell, Thomas. *Inside American Education: The Decline, the Deception, the Dogmas*. New York: The Free Press, 1993.

Sproul, R. C. *Defending your Faith: An Introduction to Apologetics*. Wheaton, IL: Crossway Books, 2003.

Sterk, Endrea (Editor). *Religion, Scholarships, & Higher Education: Perspectives, Models, and Future Prospects*. Notre Dame, IN: University of Notre Dame Press, 2002.

Thelin, John R. *A History of American Higher Education*. Baltimore, MD: The John Hopkins University Press, 2004.

Tchudi, Stephen and Diana Mitchell. *Exploring and Teaching English Language Arts*. Reading, MA: Addison Wesley Educational Publishers, 1999.

Waggoner, Robert L. *Biblical Theism vs. Secular Humanism: A Class to Train Theists to Confront Humanism*. Brentwood, TN: Erskine Theological Seminary, 2000.

Walker, Decker F. and Jonas F. Soltis. *Curriculum and Aims*. New York, NY: Teachers College Press, 1986.

Wall, Edmund (Editor). *Educational Theory: Philosophical and Political Perspectives*. Amherst, New York: Prometheus Books, 2001.

Ward, Keith. *God, Faith & the New Millennium: Christian Belief in an Age of Science*. Oxford, England: Oneworld Publications, 1998.

Warfield, Benjamin B. *The Religious Life of Theological Students*. Phillipsburg, NJ: P & R Publishing, 1992.

Whitehead, Alfred North. *The Rhythm of Education, The Aims of Education* and Other Essays. New York, NY: The Free Press, 1967.

Whitehead, John W. *Freedom of Religious Expression: Fact or Fiction? (Commentary)*. Fort Lauderdale, FL: Coral Ridge Ministries, 1984.

Winch, Christopher and John Gingell. *Key Concepts in the Philosophy of Education*. London, England: Routledge, 1999.

Wise, Russ. *Education and New Age Humanism*. Richardson, TX: Probe Ministries, 1995.

Wolterstorff, Nicholas P. *Educating for Life: Reflections on Christian Teaching and Learning*. Grand Rapids, MI: Baker Academics, 2002.

Zacharias, Ravi. *Can Man Live without God*. Nashville, TN: Word Publishing Group, a Division of Thomas Nelson, 1994.

Subject Index

—〰—

Dr. William Valmyr
Biographical Sketch

D r. William Valmyr is the founder and president of Higher Call Ministries International and serves as a professor of Religious Studies at the University of Fort Lauderdale. He also serves as an adjunct professor at various institutions of higher learning including Broward College (formerly Broward Community College), South Florida Bible College, and The Fire Institute. His passion is to train Christian leaders at churches and ministry training schools. He carries a special burden for developing and mentoring Christian leaders that will impart the Christian worldview within their sphere of influence. His careful research and study have resulted in presentations on Religious Education, Spiritual Formation and the Christian Worldview.

In the course of his professional career, Dr. Valmyr has served as a leader in various ministries including Christian Education, small groups, counseling and Youth Ministries. He is a member of the Evangelical Training Association, the American College Counseling Association and a professional member of the American Counseling Association. He is the recipient of several teaching and academic awards including, Who's Who Among America's Teachers and the United States Achievement Academy Award.

William has earned a Bachelor of Science in Psychology, a Master of Science in Educational Administration, and an Educational Specialist degree in TESOL from Nova Southeastern University; a Master of Arts degree in Christianity and Culture from Knox Theological Seminary, and a Doctor of Philosophy in Religious Education (Worldviews and Higher Education) from South Florida

Theological Seminary; and is currently completing a Doctor of Ministry (Church Ministries & Leadership) at Oral Roberts University. He is the author of *Christianity and Culture: A Christian Perspective on Worldview Development* (Xulon Press).

Dr. Valmyr is a practical teacher, minister, college professor, author, speaker, counselor and husband whose mission in life is to challenge hearts and reach the culture through the transforming power of the Word of God. He enjoys reading, writing, lecturing and spending time with his wife Marsha and daughter Meghan.

If you are interested in further information about Dr. William Valmyr, please contact Higher Call Ministries International, via E-mail at: highercallministriesintl@hotmail.com or at: P.O. Box 771325, Coral Springs, FL 33077

Breinigsville, PA USA
19 October 2009
226061BV00001B/14/P